THE QUESTION OF
SCOTLAND

DEVOLUTION
AND AFTER

TAM DALYELL

Foreword by PETER

First published in 2016 by
Birlinn Limited
West Newington House
10 Newington Road
Edinburgh
EH9 1QS

www.birlinn.co.uk

ISBN: 978 1 78027 368 6

British Library Cataloguing-in-Publication Data
A catalogue record for this book is available from the British Library

Typeset by 3btype.com
Printed and bound by Grafica Veneta (www.graficaveneta.com)

Contents

❖

Acknowledgements

❖

HUGH ANDREW, Managing Director of Birlinn, had the perceptive insight that this historical record would be of significance for those with an interest in the history of Britain between 1960 and 2015.

I extend my thanks to him for publishing this book; to Andrew Simmons, who guided it through the editorial process; and to Patricia Marshall, who copy-edited it.

Without the critical comment, love and support of my wife, Kathleen, over fifty-two years, such a book as *The Question of Scotland* could not, and indeed would not, have been written.

Tam Dalyell
The Binns
West Lothian
July 2016

Foreword

❖

TAM. ONE WORD. Instant recognition. It's a characteristic he shares with Enoch (Powell) in another generation and Boris (Johnson) in the current one, though he is very different from the other two. In fact, Tam is different full-stop; a one-off. An aristocrat, a maverick, a Labour man and a unionist to his core, he perfected over his decades in the House of Commons a potent gift for using courtesy as a weapon.

There was no deadlier deployer of the parliamentary question, oral or written. And he wielded a famous supplementary for the hapless minister who had to take his oral ones on the floor of the chamber – 'Why?' The phrase 'without fear or favour' could have been coined for him. A phone call from Tam is an event; a special occasion to be savoured.

The Question of Scotland is another special Dalyell solo. It provides a one-man spinal cord through a protracted and complicated story, the last act of which may be about to unfold as one of the multiple repercussive effects of the UK's decision to leave the European Union.

Within these pages lies much bounty for the political historian and the observer of British and Scottish politics.

Tam's diary entries can make even a meeting of the Scottish Labour Party's Executive Committee rise off the page. Linger, for example (chapter 5), on his account of such a meeting on 17 August 1974 between the two general elections of that year – the occasion when Labour's grain was cut towards devolution and, as Tam saw it, the first steps towards a sundering of the United Kingdom, the day, he wrote in his diary, when he felt 'the tartan curtain was falling all around us'.

The Question of Scotland is also rich in character. Tam is a master of the biographical vignette. He brings out not just the Westminster and Whitehall anthropologies involved but also the now mightily shrivelled Scottish Labour movement – its rhythms, its fault lines, the rivalries and the animosities of the men and women of the left who grew up during the 1930s slump or the 1940s World War and who helped shape the postwar years of mixed economy and welfare state.

I write these words but three days after the EU referendum result was declared with a palpable feeling that the United Kingdom which made me, shaped me and which commands my love and loyalty may now on a path to rupture. It makes Tam's 'Postscript' an almost unbearable read. Take a deep breath before you attempt it.

Peter Hennessy, FBA
Attlee Professor of Contemporary History,
Queen Mary, University of London
July 2016

Introduction

❖

ONE OF THE leitmotifs of Tam Dalyell's political life has been his passionate commitment to Britain and his deep understanding of the consequences of change in the constitutional arrangements of the country. However deep his feelings on the matter, he has retained a rare generosity of spirit and courtesy towards his political opponents of whatever stripe. Both this and his long career give him a depth of insight that few can match. This book is the story of how a series of short-sighted tactical adjustments, of personal feuds, of failures to comprehend an implacable and unrelenting opponent have led Britain to the edge of breakup. It is a story repeated by the struggle over Europe in British politics, a subject too on which Tam feels passionately.

His fervent and deeply held conviction that it is through partnership that we achieve progress has run like a thread through his life. It is an example from which much can be learnt in these troubled times. This book is not simply a history but a warning, a warning about what happens when we seek the quick fix over the principled solution, a warning about failure to understand the forces that lay siege to liberal democracy and to those who seek to co-opt those same forces for short term gain. Tam well understands with Edmund Burke that the displacement of a few stones can set off an avalanche of unknown consequence and duration. We would do well to ponder his words.

Hugh Andrew

1

A 'Man of the Union'

❖

IT IS BEST to be candid.

By ancestry, by conviction, by emotion and by the practical political and economic realities of the 21st century, I am a 'Man of the Union'. 'Unionist' is a term associated with the Tory Party and refers not to Scotland but to Ireland. I find Nationalism, in general, distasteful. As the late Willie Ross, Secretary of State for Scotland under Harold Wilson, once said, there are only two places for Scottish nationalism – Hampden Park, Glasgow, and Murrayfield, Edinburgh.

It was my great-grandfather, twelve times removed, Mr Edward Bruce (died 1611), who was not only the Scottish Ambassador at the Court of St James, but, more importantly, the negotiator, on the Scottish side, as to who was to succeed Elizabeth of England. The Tudor court was, to put it mildly, not the simplest – or safest – of environments. Bruce negotiated, first of all, with Sir Francis Walsingham and, more particularly, his secretary, William Davidson, who had 'handled' the execution of Mary, Queen of Scots. After Walsingham died, Bruce conferred with Lord Robert Cecil. As one can imagine, the whole issue was delicate in the extreme.

The Earl of Huntingdon had a sounder claim to the throne than the Scottish king. Moreover, Elizabeth did not countenance open discussions of her own demise, least of all in relation to James VI of Scotland, whose mother had been beheaded on her orders. But such was the skill and tact that Bruce displayed in the 1580s and 1590s that the transition in 1603 went smoothly. Bruce went to London in James's entourage, to become Master of the Rolls, actually a senior civil servant rather than a law officer. He, in turn, took Thomas Dalyell with him. This tough butter merchant and burgess of Edinburgh was his son-in-law who lived in Fetter Lane and he became one of the 'Hungrie Scots' – Scots who did well out of the fact that the Scottish king ascended the English throne. If you ask me how he made some of his money, the truth could be encapsulated in three words – 'cash for honours'.

In 1612, Edward Bruce having died the year before, Thomas returned to Scotland, bought 'The House and Lands of Bynnis' from his cousin, a member of the Livingston family, and built most of the house in which I have lived for 83 years – it was the first house to be given to the National Trust for Scotland in 1944, under the Country House Scheme.

The late John Smith, the former Labour leader and the person in charge of the failed 1979 Scottish Assembly Bill and legislation in the Commons, came to lunch at The Binns. He gazed up at the portrait of Thomas Dalyell, by the Aberdeen artist George Jamesone, and observed to his daughters, rather drily, 'He's the source of all your father's woes over the parliamentary legislation!' Thomas's son, one of few men to have escaped from the Tower of London, General Tam Dalyell, went once a year 'for to Kiss the King's hand' and to gossip as friends in adversity in the 1650s.

Subsequently, the Dalyell family would have nothing to do with the Jacobite rebellion of 1715 and the ill-fated Bonnie Prince Charlie in 1745. In the early nineteenth century, Sir John Graham Dalyell, FRS, was a teacher of Darwin, friend of Sir Walter Scott and part of the Scottish Enlightenment, which had, according to the current Professor of Medieval History at the University of St Andrews, Professor Robert Bartlett, taken off shortly after the Act of Union.

My grandfather fought at Gallipoli with the 3rd King's Own Scottish Borderers, whose regimental home is Berwick-upon-Tweed and whose company contained many Englishmen from Norham-on-Tweed and Hexham. My father was part of the Raj, his father was British Resident in Kathmandu and their family were functionaries of the East India Company over seven generations. So, by blood and conviction, I am a 'Man of the Union'.

2

First Skirmishes

IT WAS A blustery October Friday morning at the Town House in Jedburgh, where the count was taking place for the result of the 1959 general election in the Roxburgh, Selkirk and Peebles constituency, where I was standing as the Labour candidate. My opponents were the incumbent MP, Commander C.E.M. Donaldson (Conservative) and Dr John MacCormick (Liberal), the eventual runner-up. They did not exchange a word – their relationship during the campaign had been particularly acrimonious. When it was announced that Commander Donaldson had retained his seat, he came up and thanked me for putting up such a strong showing. I received 9,336 votes, many of which might have gravitated towards the Liberals, and had thereby helped to save his seat.

Then he said that, for all that MacCormick played the Scottish card, he had not done as well as the press thought he would. As a Canadian by birth, Donaldson knew all about separatist movements in francophone Canada but Britain was different – we all had the same language and had been together for over 250 years, since 1707.

Later in the morning, I had a civilised conversation with

MacCormick, who really thought he was going to win. He said he'd tried to tell voters that Scotland was getting a raw deal but they would not listen. Little wonder perhaps, because its thriving woollen mills made Hawick one of the most prosperous towns in Britain. Dr MacCormick's son, Iain, became SNP MP for Argyll and his other son, Neil, was the distinguished and charming holder of the Regius Chair of Public Law and the Law of Nature and of Nations at the University of Edinburgh and one of the brains of Scottish Nationalism. But although Dr Robert McIntyre, a popular physician, had been SNP MP for Motherwell, fleetingly for a few months in 1945, there was no indication, in 1959, that a Scottish Nationalist candidate could get near election to the House of Commons.

But then there was a largely forgotten and bizarre development which I believe sowed the seeds of trouble. MPs were paid a proverbial pittance. I personally know of Glasgow MPs at that time who would fly to London on Monday morning, get the night sleeper back to Glasgow on Monday night, fly down to London on Tuesday morning, get the night sleeper on Wednesday night, return by air on Thursday morning, and catch the night sleeper on Thursday night for the sake of saving money on London hotels, there being no accommodation allowance in those days. But most would go back to dingy digs in London on Monday, Tuesday and Wednesday nights. The result was that many Scots MPs had little better to do than to keep government members up at night, with interminable speeches, using the many procedural devices, such as Second Adjournment Debates, then allowed by House of Commons Rules. And no speeches were easier to make than those *gurning* – a good Scots word for 'complaining' – about every conceivable affront, real or imagined, concerning the state of affairs in Scotland. Thus, in those far-off days, when the Scottish press was interested in events at Westminster,[1] many Scottish MPs gained a reputation for being 'bletherers and wind bags'. Many a parliamentary hour was spent by MPs deploring the non-acceptance of Scottish bank notes by London taxi drivers – actually, a rare occurrence.

In this atmosphere of grievance and with the economic plates shifting, it was not entirely surprising that the SNP polled respectably at a by-election in the Glasgow Bridgeton constituency in 1961. Jimmy Bennett, the Labour candidate, was elected with 10,930 votes, followed by the Conservatives with 3,935, with the Scottish National Party candidate hard on their heels with 3,549. This was the taste of things to come – the first straw in the wind. The next event was the by-election in West Lothian, precipitated by the death in March 1962 of the Deputy Chief Whip of the Opposition (Labour) John Taylor, who had gone on a parliamentary visit to Tanganyika, as Tanzania then was, and acquired a tropical disease, aggravated by pleurisy. As this by-election turned out to be a pivotal moment in the rise of Scottish Nationalism, it is necessary to say something of the candidates and the special circumstances surrounding them.

The Conservative candidate was Ian Stewart, a successful Edinburgh lawyer, and a nice man, who at the 1959 general election had run up 18,083 votes. But, in April and May 1962,

---

1   *The Scotsman* had three full-time correspondents covering parliamentary affairs, as did the *Glasgow Herald*. The *Scottish Daily Mail* had Joe Haines, later to be Harold Wilson's confidant and press secretary, and, most widely read of all, the *Daily Express* had the ubiquitous Gordon Campbell.

Stewart was committed to important legal cases in the Court of Session in Edinburgh. In those days, political activity on a Sunday was counter-productive, as many electors believed that the Sabbath ought to be politics-free. So Stewart's campaign was limited to touring the towns and villages of West Lothian in his sports car on Saturdays blaring out over a loud-speaker, 'I'm not a greedy chap – I got 18,000 votes last time – give me a few more [this time].' This was hardly a politician's message for people with many problems, in particular those following the closure of the shale mines and the closure of the Woodend Colliery in Armadale, one of the few pits in Scotland producing high-grade anthracite.

Worse still for the Conservative cause was Stewart's one television appearance. May 1962 was the first occasion in Scotland, and maybe Britain, when TV had played a part in a by-election. All the candidates were interviewed in turn by Professor Esmond Wright on a sweltering afternoon at a spot overlooking Bathgate. Ian Stewart turned up in a light-coloured summer suit, a white shirt and a yellow tie, which made him appear like a photographic negative when seen on the television screen. The visual impression was doubtless but unfairly extremely damaging. All this combined to create the conditions for a lost Conservative deposit. The beneficiaries of the Conservative misfortunes were the Scottish Nationalists. The switch from Conservative to SNP support was under-standable, given that a significant number of SNP activists had been small business people, formerly members of the Conservative or rate-payers' associations. These were the 'Tartan Tories' (an epithet coined by Willie Ross later, in 1967), who wanted to punish a government which had been in power since 1951 and had become stale and scandal-prone.

Standing for the Communist Party was the general

secretary at its King Street headquarters in London, Gordon McLennan. He attracted a significant 1,511 votes. He was an impressive candidate, whose support came from Lawrence Daly, the miners' leader, one of the most gifted orators of his generation and someone I was to share many a platform with against the Vietnam War, John McLean, Secretary of the Scottish NUM living in Blackridge, and Ron Sayers, Secretary of the West Lothian Trades Council, in West Lothian. Some of McLennan's supporters, particularly Willie Collins of Blackridge, pit delegate at Woodend Colliery, Armadale, were to work hard for me during my Labour candidacy in future general elections. They all enhanced the level of political argument, at the joint hustings meetings of all five candidates.

The Liberal Candidate, David Bryce, was a cheerful, good-hearted and, I fear, politically naive young businessman. Years later, I was told that the main reason he 'threw his cap into the West Lothian ring' was to oblige a very elderly relative, who lived in Linlithgow and had supported Liberal MPs, law officers and the henchmen of Gladstone and Henry Campbell-Bannerman, who wanted to uphold the Liberal tradition.

In any by-election, it is highly desirable that a political party should consider 'horses for courses'. In 1962, the SNP chose a well-nigh ideal horse. William (Billy) Wolfe was a considerable local figure. He was born, brought up and went to school in West Lothian; he was (at that time) a popular employer at Wolfe's shovel works in Bathgate; he had been a well-liked scoutmaster and had become County Commissioner of Boy Scouts; he was a leading figure in the Scottish National Party, for whom busloads from outside West Lothian were prepared to come to canvass; he was a prominent member of the Church of Scotland; and not least he had a charming and extremely supportive wife, Mamie Dinwiddie.

Ironically, my first encounter with Billy Wolfe was at a non-political event in his home village of Torphichen, to commemorate the Knights Templar, when he tried (very nicely) to woo me away from the Labour Party to join the Scottish National Party. He expressed great disappointment that he was unable to convince me. Etched in my memory is Wolfe's reaction. He was not angry. He was not aggressive. He was simply nonplussed. It seemed to me he could not comprehend that my being proud of my Scottishness was in no way incompatible with my being a fervent supporter of the Union. He seemed incredulous that someone like me should display such a deeply held conviction that the Union was better for Scotland.

When the by-election was announced, Wolfe had the strong endorsement of two men who were to become lifelong friends of mine over the years – Bob Findlay, editor of the *West Lothian Courier* and an ex-shale miner, and his talented leader-writer, Sandy Niven, then a teacher at Bathgate Academy and later rector of Armadale Academy, who thought that an Old Etonian like me was a totally unsuitable candidate to represent a constituency which then had six major coal mines.

On the basis of my experience of going door to door canvassing, of addressing factory gate meetings and of attending 45 meetings in the evenings, in halls up and down West Lothian, I said to Will Marshall, a canny and disabled Fife miner, who was Secretary of the Scottish Labour Party, 'Will, I think the SNP are going to get 10,000 votes.' 'Tam,' he replied, 'I thought you were a man of sensible judgement – if you think that, I wonder if you have the judgement to become a Labour Member of Parliament.' Wolfe did not get 10,000 votes – he actually got 9,750.

And, finally, there was me – a highly improbable Labour candidate. An old Etonian called Tam Dalyell – only 29 years of age, a former Chairman of the University Conservative Association in the University of Cambridge, unmarried, no girlfriend, living in the big house in the middle of the constituency that was well known as the first house that the National Trust for Scotland had asked for under the Country House Scheme and with little Labour Party activity other than as Labour candidate in the Roxburgh, Selkirk and Peebles constituency in 1959. My only saving grace was that I was known to be an effective schoolteacher at Bo'ness Academy, who had been in charge of the under-15 school football team which had won the Scottish Schoolboys' Cup and had played a number of successful matches abroad. As Frank Cousins, General Secretary of the then mighty Transport and General Workers Union, put it to me, 'I have known worse reasons for being selected as a Labour candidate than running a boys' football team.'

That I was selected was on account of a combination of strange circumstances. On the unexpected death of John Taylor, the party in West Lothian had assumed that the candidate would be the extremely able Constituency Labour Party Secretary, Councillor Jimmy Boyle of East Whitburn. After weeks of dithering, Boyle, who had recently been widowed and left with two young children, had just remarried and decided he would not stand. Frantic invitations were sent out to Ian Mikardo, who had lost his seat in Reading at the general election in 1959 but who had retained his position on the National Executive Council of the party. Mikardo replied that Scottish politics was not his scene. Then approaches were made to the brilliant John Pollock, Chair of the Labour Party in Scotland. He opted to remain as headmaster of

Mainholm Academy, Ayr, with the prospect of becoming General Secretary of the Educational Institute of Scotland.

After further scratching around, the West Lothian party was left with a short leet of six. Olive Taylor, widow of John Taylor, the previous MP, was a councillor of Hemel Hempstead and West Lothian people thought they would see even less of her than they saw of her husband. She was first out with one vote. The next out was Willie Ferrier of the Foundrymen's Union, a moulder at the Atlas Steel Works in Armadale – an excellent candidate, except that he was an ex-provost and councillor in Armadale, where the town council had recently achieved national notoriety for selling the town hall's piano for a crate of whisky. The prospect of ribaldry was too much for the 162 delegates at the selection conference. The third one out was Arthur Houston, an ex-merchant navy man turned schoolteacher, whose Glaswegian views did not appeal to the east of Scotland but who, in my opinion, would have been a good MP, and who was the most generous person imaginable towards me, coming through day after day to campaign in the by-election, bringing helpers, including my future wife of over 52 years, Kathleen Wheatley.

Three candidates were left – one from the Amalgamated Engineering Union, one from the National Union of Mineworkers, and me. At the time, the AEU candidate was involved in a sticky court case in Edinburgh involving alleged corruption and although I was not aware of this some of the delegates knew about it. The NUM candidate was 63 years of age and was there because the Communist Secretary of the Scottish Miners, the redoubtable Abe Moffat, wanted him out of his office in Edinburgh's Hillside Crescent. Even so, had the AEU candidate come second, rather than third, I would have been defeated, as the majority of the NUM votes would have gone to the AEU. Mathematically, I had great fortune. Good fortune, too, that, since I had been nominated by NACODS (National Association of Colliery Overmen, Deputies and Shotfirers) Kinneil, some of the miners voted for me. Laughter is important in politics. To their temporarily frustrated General Secretary they said, 'But, Abe, Tam Dalyell was nominated by a constituent branch of our own trade Union!' As Paddy Flynn, Chairman of the Constituency Party, put it to me the following day, half joking but wholly in earnest, 'You were the least unsatisfactory candidate.'

Many eyebrows in the electorate of West Lothian were raised when they heard of the local party's choice. Most Labour voters, having gulped, reacted with something along the lines of 'Give the lad a chance. He was selected by a huge selection conference, many of whom knew him well, as a party member and local schoolteacher.' On paper, I held the Labour vote – with 21,266 votes, just over 50 per cent of the turnout – but I have often wondered how many Labour votes did drift off to the SNP, in the belief that my background was de trop. It is certainly true that Labour lost some potentially active young members, such as the future SNP County Convener, my friend Jimmy McGinley, to the SNP.

What would have happened if West Lothian had had a good, solid, orthodox Labour candidate in May 1962? Would Labour have had an even more handsome majority? The Friday morning after the by-election was a crucially important moment in my life. The election had taken place on the Thursday but the count of the votes was postponed until then for the very understandable reason that West Lothian Council did not relish paying late-night overtime to the scrutineers. The examination of the ballot boxes was leisurely and seemed interminable, and the returning officer, John

Calder, was not a man to be deprived of his 11 o'clock coffee, a kindness he extended to all his colleagues involved in the proceedings. The upshot was that I had plenty of time to chat with Billy Wolfe, the SNP candidate who was to become chairman of the party in 1969. And I talked at length with a number of his key entourage – Alex McGillivray of East Whitburn, Jimmy McGinley of Bathgate, the Kerr family of Armadale and the bank clerk, Bob Kellock of Bo'ness. As we talked, it dawned on me that they were not in the least interested in the meanderings of some university Labour clubs about home rule for Scotland. (Although there had been significant argument about the merits of Scottish home rule in the 1920s and 1930s among the Clydesiders, there was little appetite for home rule in Labour circles post-1939.) Not at all. They had what Professor Alan Alexander, current General Secretary of the Royal Society of Edinburgh, has termed 'laser-like fixation on Scottish statehood'. In no way could they be appeased. It became clear to me that any form of devolution would never, ever be acceptable to them. Statehood was what their lives were about. From that Friday morning in May 1962, I have been in what John Stuart Mill called the 'deep slumber of a decided opinion' that feeding the SNP monster is misguided.

Later in 1962, there was another Scottish by-election – this time in Glasgow Woodside, a seat held in 1959 by the Conservatives with a majority of 2,084. Although the Labour candidate, Neil Carmichael, triumphed with a majority of 1,367 to gain the seat, the Scottish Nationalists, even facing a particularly popular Liberal candidate, the *Glasgow Evening Times* journalist and columnist, Jack House, recorded 2,562 votes (House polled 5,000 in the 1962 by-election and 2,443 in the general election of 1964). Not only was this a good result but the SNP fielded a seriously attractive and articulate candidate in Sandy Niven, later headmaster of Armadale Academy.

What the by-election results for Bridgeton, West Lothian, and Glasgow Woodside combined to do was to make it apparent that casting a vote for the Scottish Nationalist Party at the 1964 general election would not necessarily be a thrown-away, useless vote. In the 1959 general election, the SNP gathered a mere 21,738 votes across Scotland. Five years later, in 1964, their vote tripled to 64,004. Although not a single seat was won, it should have been ominously clear that one might be, given time, particularly in constituencies where the SNP had made some inroads. And, in fact, at that election they achieved: 2,197 votes in South Aberdeen; 1,925 in East Aberdeenshire; 5,106 in Stirlingshire East and Clackmannan; 5,126 in Dumfries; 5,004 in West Dunbartonshire; 2,635 in East Fife; 2,366 in Glasgow Springburn; 1,600 in Glasgow Woodside; 3,522 against the Prime Minister, Sir Alec Douglas Home, in Perth and Kinross; 4,423 in Kirkcaldy; 1,657 in Rutherglen; 4,526 in Stirling and Falkirk; and a whopping 15,087 against me in West Lothian. Scottish nationalism had metamorphosed into a significant political force. What no one, other than the West Lothian Labour Party and I, realised was that it could happen sooner rather than later – and it did in Hamilton in 1967.

3

Madame Ecosse est arrivée

❖

AT THE NEXT general election, in 1966, I seriously wondered if I was for the political chop. Monday to Thursday, I had to be in London, helping to sustain a government with a single figure majority, dwindling at one point to minus two. At weekends, my wife and I, supported by an extremely loyal, numerous and vibrant constituency Labour Party, worked very hard to do what is the first and most important part of the job of any MP – to represent and look after all their constituents, whether they have voted for them or not. No meeting was too sparse to attend. No community too small to be visited. Two surgeries every Saturday. No case too trivial to command a full answer. No pothole too small to be quietly brought to the attention of the Roads Department of West Lothian County Council. Had it not been for constant local activity, West Lothian in 1966 and not Hamilton the year after might have been the first SNP spectacular victory.

In 1966, in the run-up to the election of that year, the SNP concentrated resources in West Lothian where Billy Wolfe, their most high-profile candidate, was once again standing. And 'that bloody Tam Dalyell' was the scalp that the SNP particularly wished to get. In the event, the figures for the West Lothian constituency in June 1966 were: Dalyell, T. (Labour) – 26,662; Wolfe, W.C. (SNP) – 17,955; MacKinnon, D.L. (Conservative) – 5,726; Swan, I. (Communist) – 567. Labour romped home with a Commons majority of 96. Complacency reigned. But, within the space of just a couple of months, there was to be a rude awakening.

The first of Labour's spectacular by-election own goals had its venue not in Scotland but in Wales. And, ironically, the root cause lay in the character of the prime minister. Harold Wilson was a personally kind man, who cared about individuals with whom he had worked and was exceptionally considerate when they faced adversity. Before the general election of 1966, as Leader of the Labour Party, he was in a position to know that Lady Megan Lloyd George was terminally ill but still intended to stand again in Carmarthen. The daughter of Earl David Lloyd George of Dwyfor, the chancellor who brought in the 1911 radical Budget that paved the way for the Welfare State and war-time prime minister from 1916, she had held the Carmarthen seat for Labour since the by-election in February 1957.

James Griffiths, Deputy Leader of the Labour Party and, for 30 years, miners' MP for the neighbouring constituency of Llanelli, along with Dame Sarah Barker, the formidable Yorkshire woman who was then the National Agent of the Labour Party, supported Wilson's insistence that Megan be allowed to contest her Carmarthen seat in 1966. She was returned by 9,233 votes over her Liberal opponent. However, throughout the campaign, she was too ill to appear at hustings – which took place three or four times a night in those days – and her stand-in was Gwilym Prys-Davies. So, understandably, when Megan died just weeks after the general election, Prys-Davies was anointed by the local Constituency Labour Party as their by-election candidate and endorsed by the National Executive Committee.

My friend from my undergraduate days, John Morris, now Lord Morris of Aberavon, told me that Prys-Davies might well have been a victorious Labour candidate in a general election but the truth was that, in the hurly-burly of a by-election, under intense scrutiny, he was a catastrophic candidate, blundering at public meetings and losing any confidence he might have had. Only those, like me, who have fought a highly charged by-election can fully understand the pressures on a candidate, when his or her party expects him or her to win. As Cledwyn Hughes recalled to me when I was his vice chairman of the Parliamentary Labour Party, 'Prys-Davies crumbled. But, remember, hindsight is a wonderful thing!' Besides, there was great indignation among the electors of Carmarthen on a number of other issues – in particular, the Labour council's decision to close a host of small rural primary schools in the remoter areas of the constituency. The electors of Carmarthen clearly thought that, as the Labour government had a Commons majority of almost 100, it could be 'scolded' in a by-election. The upshot was that the locally popular solicitor and President of Plaid Cymru, Gwynfor Evans, was elected on 14 July 1966 with 16,179 votes compared to Labour's 13,743, the Liberals' 8,650 and the Conservatives' 2,934 – a majority of 2,436. Carmarthen had demonstrated that a Nationalist candidate could win and that a vote for a Nationalist was not necessarily a vote squandered. Nationalism had got a toehold – the question was whether it could be repeated at a general election or would it be a short-lived victory as had been the case for the SNP at the Motherwell by-election in April 1945, when Robert McIntyre had won the seat for the Nationalists only to lose out to Labour at the general election in July of that year?

It is a matter of speculation but I have often wondered whether victory for Plaid Cymru in Carmarthen did not pave the way for the SNP victory at Hamilton. But, despite Evans's victory, it occurred to few, if any, in the Labour Party leadership that Labour could possibly be vulnerable in the by-election at Hamilton, at first sight the safest Labour seat in all Scotland.

Without doubt, Hamilton was one of a handful of by-elections in the 20th century which really mattered in the long term. To understand what happened and the causes of this self-inflicted wound for Labour, it is necessary to look at the background and context of the by-election.

In 1964, the sitting MP, Tom Fraser, a miner, first elected in 1943, had a 17,158 majority in a two-horse race over the Conservatives, which fell to 16,576 in 1966. However, having won a huge majority, the popularity of the Labour government plummeted after the chancellor, James Callaghan, announced swingeing cuts in public expenditure in July 1966. In the autumn of 1967, Harold Wilson did something that was politically catastrophic. He not only removed three members of his Cabinet but, out of the kindness of his heart, sent them to the Lords and found them what were perceived as cushy and well-remunerated posts outside politics.

On 2 November 1967, two by-elections were held. One was in Leicester South West, after Herbert Bowden, the former Chief Whip, Lord President of the Council and Commonwealth Secretary, had been eased out to become chairman of the Independent Television Authority. The other one was in Hamilton, after Tom Fraser had been offered the job of chairman of the North of Scotland Hydro-Electric Board. A by-election was held the following year in Dudley, on 28 March, where George Wigg, the constituency's MP since 1945 and Wilson's 'Security Overlord', had gone off to become chairman of the Horserace Betting Levy Board. 'Death is excusable' but constituents do not like their MP deserting them midterm for a 'cushy number' and will take vengeance, in an electoral sense, on the government which treats them so cavalierly. Labour were thrashed in all three by-elections.

Tom Fraser had been a loyal, effective and constructive junior minister at the Scottish Office during the entire period of the Attlee Government in 1945–1951. As an elected member of the Shadow Cabinet, he was entitled to a position in the incoming Wilson Cabinet in 1964. But (advised, I believe, by the head of the Home Civil Service, Sir Laurence Helsby) the prime minister decided that he would not have Fraser in the Ministry of Power, a portfolio which he had shadowed and where, as an ex-miner, he felt at home but instead would shunt him off to the Ministry of Transport – a subject of which he knew little. What I know for certain is that the Civil Service advised Wilson in October 1964 that there would have to be painful pit closures. As Minister of Transport, Fraser got a dismissive press – unjustly, in my opinion, as many of the innovations, such as the Breathalyser, for which his successor, Barbara Castle, was to take credit, had been initiated by Fraser and his permanent secretary, Sir Thomas Padmore. Fraser's 'golden son of Hamilton' image had been tarnished by the prime minister's quirky casting of his Cabinet portfolios, and the public impression was that, at Transport, Fraser was a fish out of water.

In addition to this issue of public perception, there was

another problem. Tom Fraser was the most upright of men, brought up in the Attlee traditions that Labour MPs must at all times display impeccable public behaviour. Thus, as soon as his appointment as chairman of the Hydro-Electric Board was announced, he deemed it improper to have any more involvement in Labour Party politics. So he declined to participate in any kind of farewell or thank-you to the Hamilton Constituency Labour Party. After a quarter of a century of supporting him as their Member of Parliament, members of the CLP were hurt and some were bluntly angry. I will never forget that, at about 5 p.m. on polling night in Hamilton, the late John P. Mackintosh (MP for Berwickshire and East Lothian) and I were invited in to have a cup of tea with the lady, a Labour stalwart for 40 years, who was the honorary secretary of one of the largest pensioners' groups in Hamilton. Spitting with rage, she turned to us and exploded, 'Tom Fraser treated us as if we were that *cloot*.' (In Scots, a *cloot* is a cloth used for wiping dirt off dishes.) At that moment, Mackintosh and I turned to each other with the same thought: 'I doubt Labour's had it.' Fraser's actions seemed so uncharacteristic of the really nice, decent, caring man that he was. A conversation years later confirmed to me that he thought he had to be scrupulously non-political, after his appointment to a non-politically partisan public office.

There was yet another misfortune for the Labour Party. Some weeks after the announcement of Fraser's departure for the Hydro-Electric Board, there was a meeting of the Scottish Area Executive of the National Union of Mineworkers, dominated by the Communists, the Moffat brothers, Abe and Alex, and the up-and-coming Michael McGahey, to decide who should inherit 'their' coal-miners' parliamentary seat. In those days, certain trade unions thought they had a right to certain seats. I was told by Alex Eadie, my parliamentary friend and neighbour, MP for Midlothian, a miner, and later Minister for Energy in the Wilson and Callaghan governments, and who was in a position to know, that the NUM Executive deliberately excluded two good local miners from their list, in favour of Alexander (Alec) Wilson, who was supposedly a 'fellow traveller'. This created burning resentment, not least because Wilson did not work in any of the Lanarkshire pits, but at Polkemmet in West Lothian. Moreover, it was widely believed that he was a Roman Catholic. Terrible rumours, mostly embellished and fanciful, circulated in the constituency which covered not only Hamilton, but Lesmahagow and Larkhall, towns which were the epicentre of the Orange Order in Scotland. A Roman Catholic fellow traveller put there by the grace of the Communists – it would have been impossible to dream up a more lethal political cocktail. Worse still, although Wilson, when he got to the Commons in 1970, turned out to be a decent but rather reticent colleague, his by-election speeches at meetings made me cringe – he simply mouthed the shrill platitudes of pit-head soap box meetings.

Having steamrollered the selection conference, the NUM sat back, complacently doing little in the way of door knocking and assuming the election was 'in the bag'. Such canvassing as did take place at Hamilton was done by Labour Party members from outside the constituency, including myself. We heard some alarming views. One party member of the local CLP Executive, no less, confided to me that he was 'bloody well going to vote for Winnie Woodburn' – the maiden name of the SNP candidate, Winnie Ewing, and the one by which he had known her at Glasgow University. 'Wilson,' he added, 'has been foisted on us by the NUM.'

Other members of the Hamilton CLP stayed at home and sulked.

Nor were the party leaders in any way alert to the dangers to Labour of the situation. Vividly I recollect being summoned by John Silkin, the pairing whip, to his office in the House where he demanded to know what I had been doing in Scotland the week before. When I told him I had been up to Hamilton, he asked if it was just an excuse to be at home in Scotland. I said that, in view of Labour's majority of 100, I believed I wasn't needed at Westminster and felt I could do more good in Hamilton where I could sense all was not well. Silkin dismissed this and told me I should have been attending the second reading of the Finance Bill. However, after the Hamilton by-election result, Silkin did have the grace to offer his abject apologies to me. This episode illustrates how the Labour leadership and Transport House were oblivious to what the voters in Hamilton were feeling and how they could not anticipate the tsunami that was coming their way after the SNP won Hamilton.

Having paraded the blunders of the Labour Party in the run-up to the Hamilton by-election, I have to say also that a major factor in the SNP's success was the attractiveness – both in a political and a physical sense – of their candidate. As Winnie Woodburn, she had been an active member of the Glasgow University Labour Club and she enjoyed the goodwill of talented contemporaries such as John Smith, future Labour leader, Donald Dewar (of whom so much more later in this chronicle), Jimmy Gordon (now Lord Gordon of Strathblane), STV presenter of political programmes, and Menzies Campbell, later leader of the Liberal Democrats. And, no doubt about it, she was a photographer's delight, which greatly helped in the election publicity. Yet her political message did not hold water. One of my parliamentary colleagues slipped into one of her meetings and his verdict was: 'She promises a Scottish utopia and charmingly and articulately spouts rubbish.'

Ten years later, when we were both members of the indirectly elected European Parliament, Winnie Ewing told me over a glass of wine in Strasbourg that she only reluctantly, out of duty to the SNP, agreed to be a candidate in Hamilton, adding that the party had not put up a candidate there at any previous election and that it was the last constituency in all Scotland in which they thought they could get a respectable vote. She continued to say that it was not until ten days before polling day that it began to dawn on the party that they might actually win.

Albeit that Winnie Ewing was a conscientious and hard-working local MP, she was squeezed out in the 1970 election when Hamilton returned to the Labour fold.

The somewhat delayed consequence of Carmarthen and Hamilton was that Harold Wilson was prevailed upon to set up a Royal Commission on the Constitution. Wilson told me privately that he thought it would cause trouble by giving the SNP 'too much credence' but such was the pressure on the government from Scottish MPs, who understandably were concerned about retaining their seats at the next election, that he had to 'kick the ball into touch'. He chose his friend Geoffrey Crowther to chair the commission but Crowther's untimely death in 1972 necessitated the appointment of another chairman. It is my opinion that, had Crowther lived, he would not have recommended the establishment of a Scottish assembly, as his successor, Lord Kilbrandon, did when the results of the commission were finally published in 1973. As so often happens in politics, unanticipated death can push events in unanticipated directions. It is my firm conviction that, had not Geoffrey Crowther succumbed to a heart attack in a London airport lounge in stressful travel circumstances, the political history of the UK would have been very different.

4

Playing the Scottish Card

❖

THE 1970 GENERAL election was a hard-fought contest during which the underdog Edward Heath beat the incumbent prime minister, Harold Wilson. On the morning of Friday 19 June, when most of the results had been declared, Labour MPs must have been reeling from the unexpected outcome but there would also have been a sense of relief that every Scottish Nationalist candidate had been unsuccessful. But just as we were thanking God for that, we realised we had counted our chickens before they were hatched. Late on the Friday afternoon, as a result of ballot boxes having to be collected from remote islands in the Hebrides and morning fog in the Minch, news came through that Labour had lost the Western Isles constituency to the SNP.

We need not have been entirely surprised. The incumbent Labour MP, Malcolm Macmillan, had first been elected to the House of Commons back in 1935, at the age of 22. At first, he had been extremely active, spending the summer going from island to island, staying in the houses or crofts of Labour supporters and non-supporters too – folk were attracted by his wit and found his stories amusing but, above all, they were impressed by his fluency in Gaelic, which indicated that he was one of their own.

But the truth was that, after 20 years in Parliament, Macmillan got bored. For the 15 years prior to 1970, he was a Whip's nightmare. When absent from Westminster, often for prolonged periods, he would tell us that he was in the Western Isles. And he would tell his constituents that he was detained at Westminster. For a lot of the time, it appears he was, in fact, toasting his toes at home in East Kilbride. By the 1960s, this talented and amusing colleague had lost all interest in politics and, by the time of the 1970 general election, his constituents had found him out – but the local Labour Party, much as they might have wanted to do so, were unable to ditch him. Exasperated, yet not wanting the Conservative candidate, Charles Cameron, who was the controversial local manager of a seaweed industry plant, locals instead voted for the SNP candidate Donald Stewart. A popular provost of Stornoway from 1958 to 1964 and again from 1968 to 1970, Stewart won by the slim majority of 726.

Soft-spoken, with a twinkle in his eye, Stewart and his ever-present, very kindly, Highland wife, Christina, settled into Westminster. The couple obviously enjoyed London life but were careful to tend their Hebridean roots. With his pipe filled with not entirely agreeable tobacco, he would show us his photographs of the Islands – he was a talented photographer and knowledgeable about the gardens and machair flowers of the Western Isles. But, for all his affability, it was his presence in the House of Commons that kept the nationalist flame alive. Had it been snuffed out and extinguished at the 1970 general election, I suspect political history might have been different. As it was, with just one

SNP MP, both the Heath government and the Labour leadership saw little point in wasting time and energy on a threat which they thought was dying a natural death anyway. But of course they were wrong. Perhaps they had failed to notice that the overall vote for the SNP had jumped from 128,000 in 1966 to 306,000 in 1970.

A couple of years after Stewart gained a toehold for the SNP in the Commons, a long-forgotten but, in my opinion, critically important event took place – the Dundee East by-election of March 1973. This was triggered by Edward Heath appointing the constituency's MP, George Morgan Thomson, as one of the first British Commissioners of the European Community. Just as in Hamilton, it was the same old story of an MP going off midterm to what was perceived as a cushy number.

Labour's by-election candidate was a bad choice. Fifty-one-year-old George Machin was an engineering inspector, a shop steward and a member of the Sheffield District Committee of the Amalgamated Union of Engineering Workers, the Secretary of the Sheffield Heeley Constituency Labour Party and a Member of Sheffield City Council. He would have been an acceptable MP for a Sheffield constituency.

He was the candidate in Dundee simply and solely because he was on the AUEW's parliamentary list and the union claimed their right to a constituency in Scotland, following the retirement of Cyril Bence, the AUEW-sponsored MP for East Dunbartonshire. Just as at Hamilton, a powerful union had imposed a candidate on a constituency who did not welcome him. Whereas Alec Wilson, who had fought the Hamilton by-election for Labour, had Lanarkshire roots, Machin, a Yorkshireman, had none in Dundee. In the weeks prior to the by-election, I worked my proverbial socks off in Dundee East. John Muir, the wonderfully street-wise and humorous Labour assistant organiser, who was in charge of the by-election, despatched me to Monifieth and Broughty Ferry with a benign chuckle, saying, 'The genteel part of the constituency may listen to your old Etonian vowels!' But, alas, most of them didn't. During those freezing March days, with the east wind feeling as if it was coming in directly from the Ural Mountains, I was invited in to numerous houses to hear the same complaint. 'Who does the Labour Party think we are?' 'Why do you bring in a man from South Yorkshire, who has never set foot in Dundee?' were the oft-repeated questions to which there were no convincing answers. And all this was compounded by the city Labour Party – or that part of it which was not mired in cantankerous feuding and charges of corruption – which just sat on its hands.

Somehow, by hook or by crook, through a combination of hard work by Labour Party members from around Scotland and residual loyalty to both Labour and George Thomson, Machin scraped home to a narrow victory. Eleven months later, having been left to his own devices and without the help that comes to by-election candidates, Machin lost his seat in the general election held in February 1974 to the SNP's Gordon Wilson – the only Labour candidate in Scotland to do so. Machin's mind, as well as his family, had remained in Sheffield. In spite of repeated warnings from Peter Doig, Labour MP for the neighbouring constituency of Dundee West, Machin failed to show up on many occasions when it was expected that he should and he never got round to fulfilling the promise he made at the selection meeting that he would move his home to Dundee.

The George Machin debacle had a huge consequence – it

paved the way for Gordon Wilson's entry to the House of Commons. A serious, skilful, upright, hard-nosed and determined politician, Wilson was light years away from his friend, the affable and convivial former provost of Stornoway, Donald Stewart.

Wilson was a well-respected solicitor in private practice. From 1963, shortly after he left Edinburgh University, until 1971, he had been the national secretary of the SNP, becoming executive vice chairman in 1972 and senior vice chairman in 1973. Elected at the first of the two elections in 1974, he was to hold the seat, with the help of a large personal following, who rightly perceived him as an excellent constituency member, for 13 years until 1983. Albeit somewhat taciturn – not a bad quality in a politician who wishes to be taken seriously – he earned the respect of political opponents.

Shortly before Gordon Wilson's election to the Commons, a political meteorite had struck the Labour Party in Scotland. John Rankin had contested Glasgow Pollok in 1923, 1924 and 1931, had been the MP for the old Tradeston constituency from 1945 to 1955 and had represented the new Glasgow Govan constituency ever since. In October 1973, at the age of 84, Rankin died. The last of the Red Clydesiders, the group of radical Glasgow MPs that included Jimmy Maxton and John Wheatley who had famously wanted to 'roast and toast the Tories', he had become notoriously garrulous and more than a bit odd and his electors, who had been loyal to him for 30 years, were at the end of their tether. Labour's stock in Govan – and, indeed, throughout Glasgow – was low in the autumn of 1973. Faction-riven between Left and Right, union members and professional people, Roman Catholics and Protestants, the Glasgow City Labour Party was in turmoil. The upshot was that the Govan constituency Labour Party chose a self-styled Marxist, Harry Selby, as their candidate – 'a clown of a politician', according to another Glasgow MP, the future Cabinet minister and European Commissioner Bruce Millan.

Little wonder then that, on 8 November 1973, this inner-city constituency sent SNP candidate Margo MacDonald to the House of Commons. Although this striking, good-looking PE teacher ('the Blonde Bombshell') was only to be an MP for three months, from November 1973 until February 1974, few MPs, simply by a fleeting presence in the House of Commons, can have had a greater long-term impact. She was also a huge public persona in Scotland until her death in 2014.

Despite the publication of the 'Kilbrandon Report', the position of most of the Labour Party regarding devolution on the night when ecstatic supporters were acclaiming Margo MacDonald at the Govan Town Hall can be summed up thus: We are still of the opinion that an assembly, other than a committee of the UK Parliament, would be a mere talking shop and would not attract the right calibre of member. Previous experience of assemblies which have no executive powers is that they are highly unstable in the sense that they do not endure, become merely symbolic or, in fact, secure some executive power. We reiterate our distaste for solutions which would involve the withdrawal of Scottish and Welsh Members and thereby leave the UK Parliament as a basically English Parliament.

The Labour Party in Scotland panicked. I know because, heaven help me, I was vice chairman and then chairman of the Scottish Group of Labour MPs at the time. It seemed to me and others, at the time, that the alarm bells were ringing a little loudly. On the very same night as the Govan by-election, in the Edinburgh North constituency, the chairman of the SNP, Billy Wolfe, was slumping to a disappointing defeat at the hands of Alex Fletcher, a future Conservative Under-Secretary of State for Scotland. And the Govan result was overtaken by events, in that the Christmas season followed and then, suddenly, before any kind of alternative strategy on devolution could be devised, Edward Heath unexpectedly went to the country in February 1974. The miners' strike and the three-day week dominated the campaign. And the result was that Wilson found himself prime minister of a minority Labour government.

The SNP gained six seats, four from the Conservatives and two from Labour – both of which could be interpreted to some extent in terms of local factors. One of the seats, Stirlingshire East and Clackmannan, was lost by the sitting MP, the late Dick Douglas, who had held the seat for Labour Co-op since 1970, after he had apparently been rude to the Labour councillors of Alloa and Alva.

As in so many situations, the facts are incontrovertible whereas the interpretation is not. What can never be proved or disproved is the extent to which the increase in SNP votes between elections had been determined by pledges on devolution, in general, and the machinery of government, in particular, and by matters such as housing, prices and unemployment. It was ever thus. But the point is that the sheer statistics of the rise in the SNP vote from 306,802 in 1970 to 633,180 in February 1974 weighed more heavily with Harold Wilson than they would have done with most politicians. In most matters, Wilson was neither vain nor conceited but, ever since 1957, when I was secretary of the

Edinburgh Fabian Society and I met him at Waverley Station to take him to the annual Scottish Fabian Society AGM, he would constantly remind me that he was a Fellow of the Royal Statistical Society. What mattered to the prime minister was that a series of private polls taken by MORI in January and February 1974 purported to reveal a 17–21 per cent intention of voters in Scotland to vote for the SNP.

The more than doubling of the SNP vote between the 1970 and February 1974 elections confirmed Wilson's opinion that 'something has to be done' about the Nats. The 'something has to be done factor' in fact pervades the entire devolution saga. But, time and again, the Labour and Conservative leaderships were far from clear about exactly *what* had to be done.

It had been, until the early 1970s, the settled policy of the Labour Party that there should be no giving in to the SNP. But some thought nationalist feelings had to be addressed. In the Labour Party, the most powerful of them was Alec Kitson, deputy secretary of the Transport and General Workers' Union, its representative on the National Executive Committee of the Labour Party and the party's chairman. His leading ally, women's section member of the NEC of the Labour Party, chair of the party, 1971–1972, and MP for South Lanarkshire, was Judith Hart. English by birth, education and demeanour and therefore vulnerable to the anti-English element, she feared losing her parliamentary seat to the SNP. She simply went overboard in supporting those who wanted the Labour Party to play the Scottish card. I'm not getting at Kitson or Hart, both of whom were friends of mine. It's simply that I was taught as a history undergraduate to search for the private motivations in the public actions of those in a position of power. In situations surrounding the question of what to do about the Scottish problem in 1974, we all had our own agendas. Some were hell-bent on promoting a Scottish Assembly. I, along with a considerable number of activists within the Labour Party, was dead set against it.

During the first days after the February 1974 election, there were no formal discussions within the party as to the right course to adopt in view of the SNP success. This was hardly surprising since the government's main preoccupation was getting Britain back to work after the miners' strike and the three-day week. But within two weeks everything had changed. The political arithmetic of the House of Commons meant that many decisions which would normally have been taken in a deliberative manner were hasty and rushed. I remember crowding into the House of Lords on the morning of 12 March 1974, to hear Her Majesty the Queen intoning, 'My ministers and I will initiate discussions in Scotland, and bring forward proposals for consideration.' Harmless enough. I was relaxed over lunch. At 2.30, the House sat again and, after the traditional pleasantries in which two MPs from the backbenches thanked the Queen for her Most Gracious Speech, Harold Wilson embarked on his formal speech, in which he explained the government's measures to the House of Commons and referred to 'our intended discussions' on Scotland.

So far, this was uncontroversial, though hardly welcome from my point of view. But then, out of the proverbial blue, came one of those fleeting moments which can have far-reaching, unintended consequences. Up stood a cantankerous Winifred Ewing, now back in the Commons as the newly elected MP for Moray and Nairn. Had it been a man, I doubt if the prime minister would have given way at such a moment but, ever courteous towards women, Harold Wilson did allow Mrs Ewing's intervention. She demanded 'proposals' instead of 'discussions'. With characteristic civility, Wilson assured her that 'we, on this side, believe in full consultation and discussions. We are not an authoritarian party.' And then, gratuitously, almost as an afterthought, the prime minister added, 'Of course, we shall publish a White Paper.' I was flabbergasted.

What had happened was that the prime minister, on one of the truly important occasions in the political calendar, had given an off-the-cuff assurance that his newly elected Labour government would publish not only a White Paper but also, by implication, an actual bill. Yet a few hours earlier, in the House of Lords, the Queen's Speech had mentioned little more than 'discussions' on Lord Kilbrandon's report, which had been published the previous year, and 'proposals for consideration'. Thus it came about that a Labour government, on the day of the opening of the new Parliament, and in response to a parliamentary interjection that could easily have been ignored, either had become committed to legislation on the Kilbrandon proposals or would somehow or other disown a statement made by its prime minister. Own goal! And how Mrs Ewing crowed about having extracted the promise of a bill from the prime minister!

A White Paper in name – but actually a Green Paper for discussion – was published on 3 June 1974, under the title of 'Devolution in the UK: some alternatives for discussion'. This was a hurried effort – How could it be otherwise? – suggesting assemblies for Scotland and Wales but bearing all the hallmarks of being ill-thought out and designed simply for the purposes of an imminent general election, which was on the cards on account of the government's cobbled-together majority. So it was that the undertaking for an assembly crept into the Labour manifesto for the second election of 1974, though what it amounted to was really the vague undertaking of a commitment to some sort of assembly in Edinburgh with unspecified powers and authority. The most monumental of shocks awaited the Labour Party.

During the months between the elections, the attitude of senior party officials was revealing. Willie Ross was no longer the towering, authoritative figure he had been in the 1960s but a somewhat diminished Secretary of State. He told me through gritted teeth that I ought to be loyal to party policy. The Willie Ross of a decade earlier would have said, 'No,' and that would have been it. In March 1974, Harold Wilson told me over a glass of brandy, at his home in Lord North Street one evening when I was heading back to my flat, 'Even Willie Ross says that we cannot renege on our policy so you'll just have to lump it – uneasy though I am.' He bade me a friendly but crisp goodnight and opened the door.

Jim Callaghan was sceptical, even after Govan, which he regarded as a flash in the pan that served the Scottish Labour Party right for putting up a left-wing militant-Marxist candidate, and was uninterested until he needed SNP votes to sustain his government after he became prime minister in 1976. Denis Healey was not prepared to discuss the assembly – at any rate, not with me – saying that his concern was the financial affairs of the United Kingdom.

The one member of the Cabinet who was wholeheartedly against devolution as proposed and foresaw what it might lead to was Edmund Dell, Paymaster General and a heavyweight member of the Cabinet, who, as a former ICI executive, was endowed with considerable financial acumen and experience of big industry. When I put this to Tony Crosland, at that point Secretary of State for the Environment, he responded, saying, 'Remember, Edmund was a centralising ex-Communist.' He then commented that the pro-devolution views of his other ex-Oxford pupil, Anthony Wedgwood Benn (whom he called 'Jimmy'), were 'romantic nonsense'.

It helped me greatly that my friend and ex-roommate in office 2a of the Upper Committee Corridor in the House of Commons, the Bristol MP, shortly to become the Labour Party Chief Whip, Michael Cocks, privately and later publicly described devolution as 'bollocks on stilts' – a view shared as ferociously by the colourful and hugely effective Deputy Chief Whip, the MP for Wakefield, Walter Harrison.

As for the parliamentary party, most English MPs in the mainstream of the party were not uninterested but felt that they had other things to do and that devolution would be better left to the Scots. There was a reminder from Vernon Bogdanor, Professor of Government at King's College, London, that 'Aneurin Bevan . . . deliberately resisted separate Scottish, Welsh and Northern Irish health services in 1946, insisting on a National Health Service, that benefits and burdens should depend not on geography but upon need. Is that principle now being compromised?'[1] For those on the Left, there was a strong feeling held by many that Bevan's principle should not be compromised.

---

1   Vernon Bogdanor, *Independent on Sunday*, 14.06.15. However, it should be remembered that separate legislation for each of the four countries of the UK was passed in the implementation of the 'Beveridge Report'.

5

A Bad, Bad Day

❖

TRUTH TO TELL, the months that followed until the second election in October 1974, are, for me, blurred. I remember being required to scurry into Glasgow every Saturday, as I was chairman of the Scottish Labour Group of MPs, to attend, in an ex-officio, non-voting capacity, meetings of the Scottish Executive Committee of the Labour Party. I cannot attempt to record a blow-by-blow account of all that happened – nor do I know of any participant still alive who could do so. Exasperation and ill temper were the hallmarks of the meetings. The chairman of the Scottish Labour Party, Allan Campbell McLean, a novelist from Inverness, and the full-time secretaries of the party, Jimmy McGrandle, and his successor, Peter Allison, tried their best to stop the comrades falling out with one another. Scottish Labour MPs were summoned to Westminster to support the government's wafer-thin majority and they spent any spare time at the weekend propping up their constituency position. We smelt political trouble and the dark clouds were all too obvious for those with a sense of history. Evan Luard, a research fellow at St Antony's College, Oxford, and a Labour Foreign Office minister, warned exactly what might happen – he firmly believed that not only would the prospect of a majority Labour government evaporate but Britain itself might fall apart if Scottish representation were to inevitably be reduced.

On Saturday, 22 June 1974, two major events occurred which were of huge significance for people in Scotland. First – and infinitely more important at the time not only for the public but for most members of the Scottish Executive of the Labour Party – was the fact that Scotland was playing Yugoslavia in Frankfurt in the final rounds of the World Cup. This meant that the second event – the meeting of the Scottish Executive of the Labour Party at Keir Hardie House in Glasgow – was somewhat overshadowed. The Secretary of State, Willie Ross, was very properly in Frankfurt for the soccer match and, out of 29 members of the Scottish Executive of the Labour Party, only 11 turned up.

I joined the Scottish Executive of the Labour Party only the following month, when I became chairman of the Scottish Labour Group of MPs in the House of Commons but I heard colourful and authentic descriptions of this celebrated meeting.

Ron Hayward, the General Secretary of the Labour Party, had written to the Scottish Executive urging them to accept devolution. He did so on the instigation of the prime minister and the promptings of Deputy Leader and Lord President of the Council, Edward Short. Furthermore, with the acquiescence of the National Executive, Clydebank-born John Forrester, an AUEW TASS member of the National Executive, had been despatched to Glasgow to help the vote go 'the right way' from Transport House's point of view – a decision which was squeezed through among a mass of administrative trivia.

During the meeting, it became clear that five of those members of the Scottish Executive who were present were against an assembly and five were in favour. The blandishments of Mr Forrester were more than matched by the tough eloquence of the Scottish Party Chairman, Allan Campbell McLean from Inverness, who was steadfastly opposed to an assembly. When the vote was taken, all eyes turned to the one member of the Scottish Executive not to have spoken, Mrs Sadie Hutton of Glasgow, who had drifted in after doing her morning's shopping. Loyal to her chairman and resentful of the pressure that was being put on him from Transport House, she raised her hand. So, by six votes to five, the Scottish Executive of the Labour Party reaffirmed their policy that an assembly was, as Allan Campbell McLean described it, 'irrelevant to the real needs of the people of Scotland'. Thus are momentous decisions actually made!

In retrospect, it has been claimed that, had there been a fuller turnout of members and had the Scottish football side not been encountering Yugoslavia at Frankfurt, a very different pro-assembly result would have occurred. I doubt this. On joining the Scottish Executive of the party the following month, I made enquiries among my colleagues as to which way they would have voted had they been present. Even allowing for the influential presence of 'old basso profundo' himself, as Harold Wilson affectionately called Willie Ross, my reckoning was that the 6 to 5 vote against an assembly at that moment reflected the majority feeling of the Executive. Those I consulted retrospectively confirmed that the vote was likely to have been 18 to 11 or even 19 to 10 in favour of the chairman's anti-assembly view.

It is impossible to exaggerate the long-term significance that the fluke chance of a near tie in the February 1974 election had on the attitudes of all the major parties to a delicate constitutional issue. In any electorally normal period, a party which has either won or lost at the poll has time to settle down and formulate its policies, after a lot of argument at conferences and a reasonable amount of mature reflection among the leaders of the party. There was relative calm in the House of Commons but not in the Scottish media. The narrow vote of the Scottish Executive was not a matter of huge moment to the parliamentarians, who saw it from a different perspective.

This was not the way the result was portrayed by the Scottish press, who accused the absent members of the Scottish Executive of succumbing to the lure of a soccer match. (To my certain knowledge, at least two of the press scribes who castigated the absent members of the Executive were glued to their own television sets on the Saturday, however they expressed themselves in Monday morning's papers.) 'Six silly men', screeched the *Daily Record*, apparently forgetting that Mrs Hutton was among them. Never underestimate the fierce enthusiasm with which the Scottish press have always espoused the cause of an assembly. They, as journalists, would become big fish in a small pool. Resentment in the offices of the *Daily Record* against the management of its sister paper, the *Daily Mirror* in London, was galvanic – outstripped only by the staff of BBC Scotland against BBC London Headquarters.

The following Wednesday, 26 June 1974, the National Executive Committee of the Labour Party met at Transport House. Towards the fag end of the meeting and certainly after several important Cabinet ministers had left for lunch engagements, the Scottish Executive's decision was lambasted by Alec Kitson of the Transport and General Workers' Union and Judith Hart, MP for South Lanark, essentially now a national rather than a Scottish figure since leaving the

Scottish Office as Under-Secretary of State in 1966 to become Minster of State for Commonwealth Affairs. Their colleagues on the NEC assumed that, as the only Scots on the Executive, they must know about the situation and agreed to their proposal for a recall conference of the Scottish Labour Party. The truth was that neither had very much day-to-day contact with the Labour Party in Scotland but this did not prevent them from being regarded as authorities within the NEC as far as Scottish affairs were concerned.

On 6 July 1974 I attended my first meeting as a member of the Scottish Executive Committee of the Labour Party. Confronted with a demand for a recall conference of the party, the executive, now in full attendance, felt in no position to refuse. My impression is that, had there been a larger attendance and a more decisive vote at the 22 June meeting, my colleagues would have summoned up the muscle to refuse. But defying Transport House was a major step, rendered more difficult by the unfavourable press reaction concerning the lack of attendance at the previous meeting. However, Allan McLean, other anti-assembly members and I reckoned that we could persuade a recall conference of the Scottish Labour Party to our way of thinking – against an assembly. We were wrong. We had failed to foresee the power and energy that Alec Kitson was to bring to his task. At the meeting of the NEC of the Labour Party in London, he was instrumental in pushing through a resolution recognising the desire of the people of Scotland for an elected assembly and calling for party support and government legislation. All this momentous handiwork was accomplished towards the end of the meeting, as members were beginning to leave. The slap-dash way in which decisions seem to have been made may appal many readers; in reality, however, there are extenuating circumstances in that trade union leaders and politicians are under such pressure that they tend to act hastily in matters which are not going to have immediate consequences, and which seem to have little bearing on their own activities. A Scottish assembly was by no means the most pressing matter occupying the minds of the members of the National Executive of the Labour Party.

More importantly, Alec Kitson undertook some neat lobbying to line up the major unions in Scotland behind the idea of an assembly. At the time, most trade union leaders were taking their well-earned holidays – and, even if they were not, many of their members were. Consultation with full-time trade union officers, let alone lay members such as chairmen of local committees, was negligible. For example, men of standing in the Labour movement, such as Ronald O'Byrne, Chairman of the West Lothian Labour Party and a convener of ICI shop stewards, negotiating pension rights for the entire United Kingdom with his company, heard not a word from his union (the Amalgamated Union of Engineering Workers) before their vote was cast on the undiscussed issue of an assembly; nor was an important National Union of General and Municipal Workers official, Archie Fairlie, West Lothian constituency agent, even consulted. Councillor Robert Lee of Fauldhouse, Chairman of the Council Planning Committee sighed: 'The Labour Party is on a raft, going down the river, and we will come to the rapids.' It may not have escaped your notice that all of these prominent party members, who should have been consulted, were active members of the West Lothian Party and known supporters of my views on the assembly.

Kitson had done his work well. The Scottish Executive, until then resolute and determined, met its Waterloo on

Saturday, 17 August 1974. I mused in my diary the following day on what had obviously been a crucial event to those of us involved but just how crucial to the future of the country was only – and gradually – to become clear in the months and years to come.

On Sunday 18 August, I made an unusually long entry in my diary and I reproduce it in full, as its immediacy gives something of the flavour of this very critical event, not only for the Labour Party in Scotland but for all concerned with British politics for the foreseeable future:

Yesterday, it was a bad, bad day. I picked up Ronnie [Councillor Ronald O'Byrne, Chairman of West Lothian Constituency Labour Party], in Winchburgh and he told me that he had had bad news on the AEU [Amalgamated Engineering Union] grapevine, that Alec Kitson had fixed Gavin Laird. When I arrived at the car-park, Ronnie and I bumped into Janey and Norman [Buchan]. Janey said bluntly that we [the anti-Assembly group] had had it; Alec Donnett of the NUGMW [National Union of General and Municipal Workers] had been squared! I could hardly believe it. I had a quick word with Frank [Gormill, of National Association of Colliery Overmen, Deputies and Shotfirers] who was to chair the Conference, and he said he would do his best, but he had his doubts about being able to carry the Conference.

Frank did well as always. He started by saying bluntly that the Executive would have greatly appreciated it if the NEC at Transport House had held back from making any statement on Scottish Devolution until after this Conference had been held. I clapped hard from my place on the platform, but noticed Alec [Kitson] looking embarrassed and sour; Judith [Hart] did not look too pleased either. Frank went on to tell Conference that the timing of the decision was 'most unfortunate' – I thought some pit language would have been more appropriate, but Frank has exquisite manners and is no Will Lawther of the Durham Miners, well-known for having told opponents 'Shut your Gob!'. Frank said rightly that the reason given by the NEC that it would have been helpful to this specially convened conference to know the views of the NEC was 'strange'.

I take this from the handout: 'One of the duties of the Scottish Council is to advise the National Executive on Scottish opinion in the party on a wide variety of subjects and this we do, but on this most crucial issue the National Executive decided to make their own pronouncements in advance of any advice that they might have received from the Party in Scotland.' Frank said that we were in a better position to assess Scottish opinion, and surely it would have served the interests of the Labour Movement better if the NEC had awaited the outcome of the special conference.

Then Allan McLean spoke. I thought he did well. He moved that Conference oppose the setting up of a Scottish Assembly as being irrelevant to the needs and aspirations of the Scottish people. He thought it would be an Oliver Twist situation. It would be a wonderful sounding-board for our political opponents. All the ills of the Scottish people, inflation, employment, inadequate housing, environment, juvenile delinquency or overcrowded schools would be attributed to and blamed on the lack of power vested in an Edinburgh Assembly and their subservience to Westminster. Allan and I have talked a lot together about scapegoat politics; he hammered it home. Perhaps he should not have got on to the Crofters of Drumbuie, [a cause célèbre at the time, involving greedy landlords, and a very worthy cause, but which slightly confused the argument on this particular occasion].

Jim Sillars was first to the rostrum. He's tremendously eloquent, and has a beautiful rich voice and a handsome youthful presence – but I do get irritated the way he supposes that only he, and not the rest of us, can interpret the aspirations of the Scottish People. How does Jim know that they have a deep desire for the devolution of powers from Westminster? I hardly think that people in Mauchline are queuing up, asking Jim for Devolution of Powers; more likely, they want to know why the Council has got them or their offspring so far down the housing waiting list. Then Jim went on about decentralisation. I recollect that during the South Ayrshire by-election [1970, at which Sillars was elected to Parliament] Jim gave me a mouthful on how Education in Ayrshire should never be run from Edinburgh, but from Ayr. He used to be very certain of his opinions even when he was Alex Eadie's agent, when we were working together in 1963. But yesterday he made a speech that mattered. He obviously does not like Westminster very much, and I thought many delegates were in the mood to believe the worst of most MPs. John Mackintosh, too, was effective, arguing that many decisions affecting Scotland were not taken politically by any public body. He had an odd passage about how directors of education, the inspectorate, or colleges of education were taking policy decisions. Clearly, John's Assembly is going to meddle both with the local authorities, and with the professional representation on ad hoc bodies. Ronnie [O'Byrne] went next and spoke excellently, putting the case for sorting out local government finance, which was the source of so much of the original discontent. If the local authorities had enough money for 'folk's housing repairs' to be done promptly, 'we would not be here to-day'!

Oh, Heavens, and then came Gavin Laird. He said he did not have time to prepare a speech since he had just interrupted his holiday to come to the Conference. He stumbled out that the AEU would not support Devolution simply for reasons of expediency. Gavin, who normally speaks well, produced a number of platitudes about improving the democratic process. He seems to think all the work of the House of Commons concerning Scotland is done in the two hours after midnight.

This is really a load of rubbish. George Lawson followed and as an ex Scottish Whip in the House told Gavin that we Scots had more than our share of time. George wanted to know where the demand for an Assembly was to be found. He pointed out that seventy SNP candidates had got 21.9 per cent of the vote, but this did not mean that there was an over-whelming demand for a separate Scottish set-up. Brian Wilson, our Ross and Cromarty candidate, who runs that extraordinarily successful and radical West Highland Free Press, just thought the party should square up to the challenge of the SNP and not run away, instead of sheltering under the umbrella of a Scottish Assembly. He thought it would lead to the destruction of the Labour Movement.

Then came the dagger. How Alex Donnett, believing what he does about the Assembly, will be able to look at himself in his shaving mirror, I know not. Anyhow, he trundled to that rostrum and solemnly told us that there had been a considerable amount of administrative and executive devolution in the last few years, and that he considered the time had come for making a systematic approach for a Scottish Assembly. Though Andy Forman of USDAW followed him, opposing the Assembly, I realised the game was up, and so did the whole Conference. In vain did Andy say defiantly that if a political party of the stature of the Labour Party resorted to political expediency, then we were on a very slippery slope. Andy Forman warned us that any further disillusionment could lead to Separation, if the Assembly did not produce the goods expected of it. Alec Kitson coolly told us that the NEC at Transport House were expected to give a lead, and this they had done in declaring their support for an Assembly. All too obviously it had been 'fixed' — and as Allan McLean whispered to me, we never had a chance. There was no earthly point in prolonging the agony into a Second Day, and we would be well advised to throw in the towel after lunch. Two other speeches stuck in my mind. A competent effort from John Smith saying that delegates who were pressing for devolution to a Scottish Government could not have their cake and eat it, by insisting that they keep the office of Secretary of State for Scotland, and all seventy-one MPs. The other was by Willie Mack, the delegate from Maryhill. Willie said that he would vote for the Assembly, without fully understanding what it was all about. 'But if you fail to make it work, you will have destroyed the Scottish Labour Party, and the national Labour Party will be in perpetual Opposition and eventual decline.' Willie added, 'If a Scottish assembly is to be the answer to the problems confronting us, please don't put it up as a vote catcher, and then run away from it. This is one of the reasons why political democracy is treated with contempt by the man in the street. He doesn't believe you. You make promises and don't keep them, and the sort of devolution I would like to see is that which brings for ordinary people policies which eliminate fear of want, bad housing, and fear of minority oppression. But I am very much afraid that unless we deal with these problems on a national level, no Scottish Assembly will save the Labour Party.'

I was itching to speak but as a member of the Executive had to sit silent on the platform; I told Allan towards the end that it was a basic error to conclude that if one only adopts Nationalist-type policies, all will be well. Things don't follow like that at all. The tartan curtain was falling all around us. There was no point in calling for a card vote, (though thinking about it later I believe we made a bad mistake not to) for we would have been beaten. Nor did I realise until last night that the AUEW delegation had divided 8:6 for the Assembly, with several anti-Assembly absences. Oh, Lord, how are decisions made in the Labour Party? Ironically, I bet the SNP chances have been greatly helped by the Labour Party in Scotland having to dance to the SNP tune. Devolution is little more than a political life jacket – and a life jacket, what's more, that will not inflate at the right time, as John Burns of West Lothian Constituency Labour Party acidly retorted to me.

After the Conference, I took Norman Crowther-Hunt [Minister of State in Wilson's 1974–76 government] home for the night. We talked in the car and later, and he is very charming. But I am far from convinced that he has his feet on the ground. I am conscious that for all his soothing words that all will be well, and that we should not worry, he neither knows us Scots, nor our history of faction; in fact, I sense that he regards us as interesting guinea-pigs on which to practise his constitutional experiments. He is obviously very close to Harold Wilson, and will play a vital part in the coming months and years, in shaping these ideas. The real trouble is that he thinks that the SNP exists because people want a different constitutional set-up; Ronnie and I know the SNP flourishes on account of the greed of the people for North Sea oil revenues, disgust at local council corruption scandals, stirring up Rangers supporters' clubs by Orangemen because there are too many Catholics in the Labour Party, and a host of other matters, which are well known to those of us who struggle along in the gutter of political life, but which are somewhat novel, if known at all, in Oxford University Common Rooms frequented by Norman. But as Ronnie said, 'He's a rare talker!'

Archie [Fairlie – West Lothian agent at elections, and full-time officer of the National Union of General and Municipal Workers] told me he was disgusted, but that the trouble was that the Unions did not know the SNP as well as we do in West Lothian, and that nothing would appease them. He thinks Alex's attitude is a lot to do with the Union leadership.

As Mr Willie Mack of Maryhill had had the foresight to point out, he and many other delegates did not know what devolution really meant. Extravagant pledges, however, had been given, and there was a commitment for a Scottish Assembly, so he supposed he ought to go along with it.

On Wednesday, 21 August, a subcommittee of the National Executive Committee of the Labour Party met and decided on a paper to be drawn up. The wording was largely left to Mr Geoff Bish, research secretary at Transport House, and Mr Philip Wyatt, secretary of a working party of the NEC. Their report was published with the imprimatur of the Home Policy Committee of the NEC on 5 September 1974. The document contained much that was unexceptionable in the light of what had happened:

> We propose the creation of directly elected Assemblies for Scotland and Wales. We have of course an equal commitment to democratic accountability of government and of equality of political rights in the English regions . . . An essential element of our policy for both Scotland and Wales is the retention of their existing number of MPs at Westminster, and the maintenance of both the posts of Secretary of State for Scotland and for Wales in the Cabinet.

There would be a block financial allocation and regional imbalance of areas of industrial decline had to be redressed. There was, however, one sentence in the document of 5 September which was squint, mistyped and from which there was obviously an erasure, unusual in documents of this nature which are put out for the benefit of the press. Yet this sentence was of thunderous significance. It read:

> It was the Labour Party in Scotland, the party of Keir Hardie, which in 1958 reaffirmed its support for the principle of maximum self-government for Scotland consistent with remaining within the United Kingdom; it was [erasure and missing a double-spaced line of typescript] the Scottish Council of Labour which, in 1974, after an open, honest debate, overwhelmingly called for an elected Scottish Assembly with legislative powers.

The press reports on Sunday, 18 and, Monday, 19 August 1974 make it clear that the delegates did not realise that on Saturday they had called for a legislative assembly – most of them were under the impression that they had called for a super-local authority. The crucial word 'legislative' had been deftly inserted into the press handout and was repeated in the White Paper on devolution published on 17 September 1974, the day before, Harold Wilson announced, as prime minister, that he was calling a general election.

6

A Super-Local Authority
for Scotland?

❖

THE RESULTS OF the October 1974 general election, which gave Labour a wafer-thin majority of three, were highly – if unevenly – favourable to the SNP and confirmed Scottish nationalism as a central issue in British politics. Whereas, in February 1974, Donald Stewart had been joined by Winifred Ewing (Moray and Nairn), Douglas Henderson (Aberdeenshire East), Iain MacCormick (Argyll), George Reid (Stirlingshire East and Clackmannan), Hamish Watt (Banffshire) and Gordon Wilson (Dundee East), in October 1974, they were joined by four more – Margaret Bain (Dunbartonshire East), Douglas Crawford (Perth and East Perthshire), George Thompson (Galloway) and Andrew Welsh (Angus South).

Unlike the Heath government in 1970, which was confronted by only one Scottish National MP who had strayed in from the Western Isles, this time the government clearly had to do something. The case for the status quo against separation had to be robustly made and could no longer go on by default. Action had to be taken.

On the Monday following the general election, the Scottish Group of Labour MPs held a press conference in Keir Hardie House in Glasgow. As chairman of the group, I assented to the proposition by a journalist that Labour would not go back on the campaign promise for a Scottish assembly and was duly reported as having done so. Moreover, I was correctly reported as having said that the Secretary of State should make haste and produce the assembly as soon as possible. I mention this press conference in some detail as, for years afterwards, Willie Ross and other pro-devolution colleagues would not allow me to forget it. In my position as chairman, I had reported the consensus of the group which, of course, I did not share and which was a fact known to everyone.

My side of the story is, however, rather simple. I was most disappointed by the 17 August conference result. The press statement of 5 September occurred when I was snatching my only three days' holiday of 1974 and, moreover, it did not highlight the point about the legislative nature of the assembly. Possibly I ought to have read the White Paper carefully but, since it was not physically in our possession when the election balloon went up, I did not. Nor, because one has a million other things to do in the course of a hectic election campaign, did I read the party manifesto, which repeated the White Paper pledge, before polling day. In the 48 hours after the result of the poll, I caught up on lost sleep and still had not read the White Paper by the time I faced the press on the Monday. I really imagined I was endorsing the super-local authority, which we understood had been agreed on 17 August. So did most of my colleagues.

For suggesting that the assembly should be produced quickly, I make not the slightest apology. If one was going to have an assembly which was essentially a super-local authority and in no way a legislative body, obviously it should have been introduced quickly. Indeed, it could have been done quickly since the current restructuring of local government into a two-tier system of regions and districts, as recommended in the Royal Commission chaired by my father-in-law, Lord Wheatley, could at that stage have been frozen in its tracks. But what would just have been possible in November 1974 was no longer so the following year. A super-local authority for Scotland could have been on the statute book by then since there would have been none of the problems attendant on a subordinate parliament. The truth was that those who wanted a Scottish parliament had inserted the word 'legislative' and had subtly used a one-way ratchet to achieve their wishes or at least a significant move in the direction of their wishes.

In 1974, the promise of Scottish and Welsh assemblies appeared harmless enough in London's eyes. It did not seem to cost too much. It seemed a neat enough solution to a worrying problem; if there was the widespread impression in Scotland that what had been promised was in effect a form of super-local government, that impression was almost universal south of the border. The confusion was easily explained. In Scotland, as elsewhere, the whole argument had been conducted up to that time in terms of over-easy slogans, trundled out as the needs of each politician's speech required. Tragically, little thought had even then been devoted to thinking the problem through in any serious manner. Phrases and catchwords were devised, with the following morning's headlines in an excitable Scottish press as the major consideration.

Following the election, the Labour government, grappling with the economic crisis, was paralysed for some months in regard to what should be done about the devolution pledge.

A petulant prime minister, mired in more pressing concerns arising from the wafer-thin Commons majority and day-to-day existence of his government, eventually got round to asking his ever-loyal Lord President of the Council, Ted Short, to take charge of the process, assisted by Harry Ewing, a junior minister in the Scottish Office.

Years later, when I was one of Short's four choices for the conferment of an honorary degree, on his retirement as chancellor of the University of Northumbria, he told me, 'I never wanted to be given responsibility for devolution. I took it simply to oblige Harold Wilson. I knew it would be difficult. I did not realise how difficult. And my Constituency Labour Party, in Central Newcastle were beginning to ask, "If you are giving the Scots all these advantages, what about us?"'

Short was involved in chairing important Cabinet committees and had responsibilities across the whole range of government so he put devolution and the knotty problems which crawled out from beneath the stones towards the bottom of his priorities. Short was my friend and I would phone him on a monthly basis at his home in Northumberland, until his death in 2012, but his shade will forgive me for recording that he could not really be bothered with the problems brought by tiresome Scots. Most of the day-to-day work on devolution was handed over to a young researcher, Vicky Kidd. I wrote in my diary at the time that I thought this opinionated young lady knew little about Scotland – though she thought she knew everything. Her musings were of little worth and I say this simply to convey the startlingly casual approach of the Labour government, which was immersed in more pressing matters than devolution.

Wilson became aware of Short's attitude and soon realised that Harry Ewing was not up to the intellectually challenging task of dealing with complex constitutional affairs and appointed Gerry Fowler, an ex-Oxford Craven Scholar and MP for The Wrekin, as Minister of State in the Privy Council Office, to deal with the thorny problems that devolution presented.

Fowler worked fast and, on Monday, 6 January 1975, he and Ewing came to a meeting of the housing subcommittee of the Scottish Council of the Labour Party at Keir Hardie House in Glasgow. It was a filthy winter's night and only nine souls were present in all. Out of the blue, Fowler started making references to what a Scottish prime minister and a Scottish Cabinet would be likely to do in relation to housing policy. At that moment, it dawned on me for the first time – and on others, such as Allan McLean, Party Chairman in Scotland – that ministers were thinking in terms of a prime minister of Scotland and the whole paraphernalia of a Cabinet system.

After the Christmas recess, when I returned to the House of Commons and conveyed these tidings about a Scottish prime minister to my parliamentary colleagues, I was met by an incredulous Bob Mellish, Chief Whip of the Labour Party, who laughed and said, 'You're bloody joking! That'll be the day, a prime minister of Scotland – Bermondsey will be wanting me to be prime minister of bleeding London!' I record this ribaldry as evidence that the Labour Party Commons managers had not the slightest notion of what their own Lord President of the Council and his colleagues were up to.

I will spare the reader the details of the cascade of speeches I was to make on the subject in and out of the House of Commons. But it is worth mentioning one of them – less for its content than for the reaction that it provoked after Ted Short had read a full account of it in *The Times*, on 3 February

1975. I was correctly reported as saying that I had been acutely unhappy the year before about the possibility of there being an assembly but that I had accepted that it was as far as we could go without breaking up the United Kingdom. 'It now seems that the Government is prepared to go much farther than the original contract with our electors.' *The Times* quoted me as pointing out that the trade unions had insisted that trade and industry should be excluded from the power of a Scottish assembly and that these responsibilities had now been given to the Secretary of State for Scotland. However, the more such powers were given to an assembly, the more swiftly would it lead to the break-up of the United Kingdom. I was quoted as having pointed out that the Scottish Executive of the Labour Party had last voted by 2 to 1 against the assembly having powers to raise revenue: 'And, even, now, when it comes to paying higher taxation than people in England, are we quite sure that people living in Scotland would be happy to oblige? It may be different when it comes to the reality of coughing up. The belief that Scotland is a nation comfortable with rates of tax higher than the UK has yet to be put to the test.' And I came to realise that funnelling further funds and further fiscal powers to Holyrood from Westminster is an ineffective way of stemming the nationalist tide.

Nor was it my understanding that there should be a Scottish Cabinet government, with the probability of a Scottish prime minister, backed by a ministerial team. Once you had this, you would have a situation where every ill, real or imagined, would be blamed on the assembly not having enough power. And the same would happen if Westminster had the power of veto and dared to use it. If Scots had their own assembly with strong powers, I believed, we could hardly claim the right to keep 71 MPs at Westminster and a Secretary of State in the Cabinet.

I refer to this not to boast of my own prescience – for, in truth, I was merely stating what was obvious to anyone who cared to think about the topic in any depth – but because my remarks provoked anger of thermonuclear intensity on the part of Ted Short. And since, even then, it should have been obvious that my points were of considerable substance and were, indeed, precisely some of the very rocks on which the Scotland and Wales Bill was to perish, it could hardly have been the irritation that senior ministers feel when their time is being needlessly wasted. What was obvious, both in interviews in his room as Leader of the House and from the debate of 3 February 1975 in the Commons Chamber, was that Short was acutely uncomfortable and was beginning to understand the enormity of the potholes in his brief. He could not be talked to. And it is no good saying that Ted Short was never talkable to. As Chief Whip, as Postmaster-General and as Secretary of State for Education, it was certainly possible to have a dialogue with him. On devolution, it was quite impossible. What had changed? To answer this question, before resuming the narrative, it is necessary to digress, as so much that follows depends on understanding the state of mind of Edward Short.

The temptations facing ministers given responsibility for items in their party's programme are extremely seductive. Honourably, they want to do a job well. As human beings, they rejoice at the opportunity of leaving their mark on history – again, not a dishonourable motive in itself. They have a vested interest of the mind in implementing legislation for change. Though perhaps his parliamentary colleagues ought to have known better, few people guessed in October

1974, when Harold Wilson handed the key role of devolution supremo to Edward Short, that he would be other than a critical senior minister, objective in his approach, ready to listen to argument and keen to display all the caution which was to be expected from a Tyneside MP on this issue. Yet, within weeks of his getting the job, it was clear that Short's mind was no longer open to the merits of the issue, even though little discussion on it had taken place in the Labour Party as a whole. Gone was the caution he had displayed on the subject during the general election when he visited Scotland. Short had seen his chance to perform a political task of historical significance, to give his name to history, as any of us might, and had suddenly become an ardent devolutionist, positively messianic in the cause of an assembly in Edinburgh. Anyone who pointed out those very difficulties on which the Scotland and Wales Bill was eventually to founder got short shrift and was firmly informed that 'the status quo is not an option'! Yet, eighteen months later, soon after he had ceased to be Lord President of the Council and a government minister and had become Lord Glenamara, he was telling the North-East Development Council, of which he had become chairman, that their duty was to watch devolution like a hawk.

My purpose in referring to these events is not to make a criticism of an old friend of nearly twenty years but to point out that it is in the nature of ministers, in the British system of government, to take action and to neglect the possible merits of inaction for no better reason than that they find themselves in the driving seat. Exactly the same happened when Michael Foot inherited Ted Short's job in April 1976. Close political friends of Michael Foot had little idea that he was an enthusiastic supporter of devolution. As Aneurin

Bevan's sympathetic biographer, it was assumed that he shared Bevan's distaste for anything to do with Welsh nationalism or giving in to demands on an ethnic basis. Both Aneurin Bevan's widow, Jennie Lee, and his loyal PPS, Donald Bruce, later Lord Bruce of Donington, were dismayed by Michael Foot's espousal of the devolution cause. My impression was that this considerable writer and polemicist, who had a real sense of the past, also wanted to leave his mark on history and saw the successful pilotage of a Scotland and Wales Bill through Parliament as a triumphant note on which to terminate a remarkable career.

Despite the fact that it was now clearly on the agenda, the truth is that, for the first 18 months of the new Labour government, differences of opinion abounded. Clear policy was there none. Devolution drifted. Politicians ran around like headless chickens. But with 11 Scottish Nationalist MPs, whose support might be critical in sustaining the government, it was clear that a grip had to be taken on the situation. So, when Harold Wilson unexpectedly announced in March 1976 that he was stepping down, the incoming prime minister, Jim Callaghan, took the opportunity to shunt (a not-unwilling) Ted Short, to the chairmanship of Cable and Wireless, as Lord Glenamara. This meant that Michael Foot, as the incoming Lord President of the Council, inherited responsibility for devolution. Now Foot was even less of a detail politician than Short. So Callaghan promoted John Smith (MP for North Lanarkshire) from being Minister of State at the Department of Energy, where he had shone as a decisive operator, to Minister of State in the Privy Council Office, with the specific task of taking the Scotland and Wales Bill through the House of Commons.

Callaghan could not have made a more astute choice. Smith was an exceedingly able lawyer, phenomenally quick at mastering a brief – and very acceptable to his parliamentary colleagues, across the whole spectrum of the Labour Party. As a right-winger, he could be jovial with the hard Left, such as Dennis Skinner and Bob Cryer, who liked him personally. It also helped that Smith, a pro-European had, like me, voted for Callaghan and not Roy Jenkins in the recent leadership election.

Furthermore, Smith was allocated two of the cleverest civil servants of their generation, Sir John Garlick and Sir Michael Quinlan, from the Ministry of Defence. Following the failure of the Scotland and Wales Bill in 1977, it was decided that separate legislation (The Scotland Bill and The Wales Bill which were very different from each other) would be a better way to go. After his retirement as Permanent Secretary at MoD, Sir Michael Quinlan told me that the Scotland Bill had been 'cobbled together'. Smith, by no means an unduly ambitious politician, saw that, if he did the prime minister's bidding in coping with the Scotland Bill, he would then be eligible for the Cabinet. From an early stage, it was clear to me that Smith, a lawyer by training, was thriving in the challenge of a difficult brief. As the bill drooled on and on, I became even more convinced that he was James Callaghan's 'gifted attorney'.

The truth of what John Smith really felt about devolution will never be known for certain. His memory is called in aid by supporters of the Edinburgh parliament when recollecting that Smith famously used the phrase 'the settled will of the Scottish people'. My clear memory is that when, in 1974, he was the Parliamentary Under Secretary of State for Energy and then justifiably promoted to be Minister of State, working under Tony Benn, as Secretary of State for Energy, he would point out that the North Sea oil industry depended on not only workers and support from Aberdeen but also from Teesside, Hull and Lowestoft. He was scathing about the SNP slogan 'It's Scotland's oil!' I don't claim that he was against an assembly in Edinburgh. I do claim that Smith had not thought very much about the issue. After all, the SNP had fared badly in North Lanarkshire, where his predecessor, Peggy Herbison, a former chairman of the Labour Party, was loved and unassailable. The SNP was simply not regarded as any kind of threat there. In 2014, when I was being interviewed in depth on the BBC's *Newsnight*, I asked the distinguished presenter, Kirsty Wark, whether she thought Smith, a close friend, really believed in devolution, she replied, 'I wonder, I wonder. I have always wondered.'

Smith's attitude to me was not that my criticisms of the Scotland Bill were groundless but later that I was, as he cheerfully put it, 'a pain in the arse.' When I wrote John Smith's obituary for the *Independent* in 1994, I asserted that he did not necessarily believe in devolution but was carrying out a task, quite honourably, on behalf of the Labour government. I was never challenged over this opinion.

At this point, allow me to fast-forward 35 years. A letter, written by Mike Elrick, the former press officer to John Smith, 1992–94, appeared in *The Scotsman* on 11 September 2014 and it clearly illuminates Smith's attitude towards independence.

This year marks 20 years since the death of Labour leader John Smith, a politician widely seen as decent, honest and truthful.

As one of the architects of Scotland's devolution settlement which led to the creation of the Holyrood parliament in 1999, he took deep pride in Scotland, his own Scottishness, but also Scotland's continued relevance in the United Kingdom.

Had he lived to see the current independence referendum, he would have respected the right of Yes campaigners to seek an independent state but would have rejected their insistence that Scots must be forced to choose between Scotland and the UK.

He would have been dismayed at how the referendum has divided Scots and would have objected to the First Minister's portrayal of the debate as 'Team Scotland' v 'Team Westminster'.

John was very much a Westminster man, but a Scottish one who believed passionately that the fight for social justice was one that should be pursued across the UK if it was to succeed.

In the 1970s, he argued that turning the clock back to 1707 and breaking up the close economic, political and social interconnections that have been created across these isles in the last three centuries would be 'an act of spectacular folly'.

I have no doubt were he with us today, as a proud Scot, he would have actively and vociferously campaigned for a No vote on 18 September.

7

Devolution: The End of Britain?

❖

A CHANGE IN my political life occurred which, ironically, was to make it easier for me to challenge the policy of devolution. In the spring of 1976, the decision was made that Labour would send a delegation, as Conservatives and Liberals had already done, to the indirectly elected European Parliament meeting in Strasbourg, Luxembourg and Brussels. Harold Wilson and James Callaghan, then Foreign Secretary, decided rightly that the former Foreign Secretary, Michael Stewart, should lead the Labour contingent. They designated me as Deputy Leader ostensibly because I was then Chairman of the Parliamentary Labour Party backbench Foreign Affairs Group but, in reality, because they wanted me out of Westminster, knowing that I would be awkward and trouble-some during the passage of the Scotland Bill. As it turned out, unforeseen by anybody including me, they miscalculated, as I could fly back to London for any day on which the Scotland and Wales Bill (1976) was being discussed. Because I determined never to be out of the Chamber, while I was in the Palace of Westminster precinct, those pro-Scottish Assembly Scottish MPs, were exasperated that they could not get hold of me to put the pressure on in spades. Others, perhaps the majority of Scottish Labour MPs, were delighted that I was doing their dirty washing for them. Had I in the years 1976–1978 been full time at Westminster, I doubt that I would have succumbed to loud-mouthed colleagues, lecturing me on party loyalty. As it was, I was absent on duty, serving on the Budgets Committee of the European Parliament – and finding time to do the first drafts of my book, *Devolution: The End of Britain?* which was published in 1977. The book was the joint idea of myself and Graham Greene, then managing director of Jonathan Cape, and the editing was assigned to Jeremy Lewis, later well-known as a literary critic of distinction. I also had the experience of going on three separate days to the Melrose home of Hugh Trevor-Roper, Professor of Modern History at Oxford. Not even as an undergraduate in Cambridge did I have such a rigorous going-over.

In retrospect, perhaps one of the reasons I got away with opposing government policy was down to colleagues feeling something like, 'Well, at least Tam Dalyell has written a book on the subject. The so-and-so may have thought it through more than the rest of us.'

Absolutely crucially – its importance cannot be overstressed – I was the ringleader of a group of 43 Labour MPs who, either by vote or by principled abstention, on 22 February 1977, declined to support a government vote to 'guillotine the bill' – in other words, to restrict the time for debate during the passage of the bill through the House of Commons. This meant that, clause by clause, sub-clause by sub-clause, the Scotland Bill Committee Stage had to be taken on the Floor of the House. Foot was furious. Smith pretended to be furious but actually relished the opportunity, I think, at that point, afforded to a young minister to show off his skills, hour after hour from the frontbench. Wily old prime minister that he was, Callaghan would be perfectly happy to let Enoch Powell, George Cunningham, the Dunfermline-born MP for Islington South, and me, with spasmodic help from others such as the young Welsh red-headed MP, Neil Kinnock, chunter on and on, while he and Denis Healey continued to try to steady the government and get it on a sounder economic keel. The Scotland and Wales Bill, the guillotine having been refused, occupied some 47 parliamentary days on the floor of the House until it was finally withdrawn.

When my book was published in the autumn of 1977, Hugh Trevor-Roper contributed a foreword, which shows such remarkable prescience that I reproduce a large chunk of it here:

All those who believe in Great Britain and its continued existence, now threatened, should be grateful to Mr Tam Dalyell, Labour Member of Parliament for West Lothian, the author of this book. Many others in our country – the vast majority, I believe – wish to preserve its unity; but too many of that majority either do not think at all about the essential nature and conditions of such unity, or do not think clearly, or lack either the basis of factual knowledge on which to reason or the courage to resist an apparently irresistible tide. If Great Britain should be dismantled, posterity will know where to lay the blame. If that sorry fate should be avoided, and the tide turned, it should know whom to thank. In particular, it should thank Mr Dalyell.

I say this in full knowledge that hundreds of British people have spoken up, rationally and clearly, against the folly of the present Government's Bill for the devolution of legislation in Scotland and Wales. They have shown how that project was hatched out of electoral expediency, fed by the irresponsible publicity of the media, allowed to grow through public indifference to what seems, and is, an irrelevant exercise, and nearly carried through by ordinary Parliamentary management. But the voices of these critics would all have been ineffective against the brute force of Parliamentary mathematics had not twenty-two Labour MPs had the courage to defy their whips and vote against their own party in a crucial debate. By that rebellion they denied to their own Government the power which it sought to curtail inconvenient debate and force its undigested bill through the House of Commons.

To oppose and defeat one's own party on a legislative programme declared by it to be of central importance is a very serious act of defiance, which no MP undertakes without an overwhelming conviction of its necessity. It also requires courage. I can think of no parallel to the action of those twenty-two MPs on 22 February 1977 since the debate, on 7 May 1940, which persuaded Neville Chamberlain to resign. But would all those twenty-two MPs have been willing to act as they did without the consistent well-informed speeches and incessant activity of Mr Dalyell?

A cardinal belief of those who oppose the project is that such devolution is not only pointless, in that it will solve no real problem, and harmful, in that it will increase the economic cost of Scottish administration, but also unworkable and can only lead, through inevitable friction, to the ultimate disintegration of the United Kingdom. This view is shared by the Scottish National Party, which voted for the Bill precisely because they believed that it would lead to that result which the Government promised that it would prevent. For the same reason, they will vote for the new and separate Scotland and Wales Bills again.

When two opposed parties insist that the same measure will lead to opposite results, one of them at least must be wrong, and we and our posterity, who will be the victims of any mistake, have a right to expect rational arguments, not merely undocumented paternal assurances, from those who prophesy our salvation. So far we have never heard, from the supporters of the Devolution Bill, any rational demonstration that their project, or any variant of it, will bring any administrative or economic benefit to the people of Scotland or of Great Britain; nor have we heard any rational reply to the specific and concrete objections which have already been made against it. As Mr Dalyell points out, Ministers have shown consistent unwillingness to discuss these questions. They have preferred to rely on vague assurances and – as they hoped – docile Parliamentary votes. Believing that, in politics, a week is a long time, they have behaved as if, for the sake of a few more votes in the immediately foreseeable future, a union of three centuries can be lightly gambled away.

History takes terrible revenges on such short views. There is a momentum in politics more powerful than the hands of those who release it. Great states have been unmade by the uncontrollable consequences of ill-considered decisions made to secure immediate petty gains or to postpone immediate petty losses. The unity of Great Britain, its continuance as Great Britain, is a matter which concerns all British people, English as well as Scots and Welsh. The Devolution Bill, which the courage of a few Parliamentary rebels stopped in its apparently well-oiled tracks on 22 February 1977, will, we are told, be presented to Parliament again, in the form of separate Bills for Scotland and Wales with only cosmetic changes from the original Bill fully described in Mr Dalyell's book; and this time, with the aid of a little judicious horse-trading, Mr Michael Foot may perhaps get his psephological sums to come out. Therefore it is essential that the true facts about Scottish government and the Scottish economy, and the real implications of the Bill, be fully ventilated and understood, before we are carried away by what may prove an irreversible process. Mr Dalyell's aim, in this book, is to set out those facts and those implications. His arguments are, I believe, unanswerable. If not, let them be answered.

Apart from some Scots MPs, nervous about holding their seats, and Michael Foot, the PLP was more than content, in private, that the House of Commons should carry on discussing devolution after the Scotland and Wales Bills were withdrawn. The constitutional problems of Scotland were secondary in their priorities. When one of my Scottish colleagues, Dennis Canavan, an ardent pro-devolutionist, went to the chairman, Jack Dormand (MP for Easington), demanding that I be disciplined for what he saw as sabotaging party policy, Dormand replied, 'What? Discipline the man who's doing our dirty washing?'

As the days progressed in 1977 and parliamentary discussion on the floor of the House dragged on, never a session went by without hitherto unforeseen issues emerging from the undergrowth – 'Creepy crawly creatures emerge from under the stones,' as Enoch Powell colourfully but accurately put it. But, despite this, in November of that year, separate Scotland and Wales Bills were introduced, the guillotine motion was won and a Scottish assembly was back on the agenda.

To their credit, supporters of the SNP have always had a far more realistic and far-sighted attitude towards the establishment of an assembly in Edinburgh than their pro-devolution opponents – they have campaigned for devolution on the very reasonable grounds that an assembly, in itself an uneasy compromise, would be unworkable and that the resulting frustration and sense of grievance on the part of its members would inevitably push them into demanding a still greater degree of autonomy for Scotland and, eventually, complete independence from the United Kingdom. Far from satisfying nationalist aspirations, an assembly with limited powers – not least in the crucial area of finance – would only create new problems and aggravate old grievances. Ironically enough, its very existence would bring about the situation it was designed to avoid.

As a subordinate parliament in a unitary state, the Edinburgh assembly would soon find itself in an impossible position. And, as we have seen, in reality, it would remain financially dependent on Westminster. And, despite the government's neat, theoretical distinction between 'devolved' and 'reserved' areas of legislation, it would, in fact, be impossible to separate specifically 'Scottish' issues from those affecting the United Kingdom as a whole. Conflict between Westminster and the new assembly would be inevitable, particularly if the governments in London and Edinburgh were of different political persuasion. Members of the assembly, from all points on the political spectrum, would be more than human if, having once tasted power, they did not come to resent the limitations imposed upon them and to demand greater powers for themselves. It's hard to believe that many of those who blithely advocated the setting up of a Scottish assembly cannot have thought out the full implications of such a step. A parliament is, by definition, a very different kind of institution from a local authority or even a regional authority and inevitably arouses far greater expectations both in its members and those who vote for it – an unworkable and essentially frustrated assembly is a recipe for disaster. It was the impracticability of the proposed assembly and its potentially fraught relationship with Westminster that have always bothered me.

The assembly was, I thought in 1977, a constitutional impossibility. A fundamental error on the part of those who advocated an Edinburgh assembly – whether out of self-interest, political expediency or a genuine belief that to do so was to align oneself with the mainstream of enlightened thought – is the assumption that is possible to establish a subordinate legislative assembly in a unitary parliamentary state like Britain and that an assembly in Edinburgh can be thought of in much the same way as existing elected bodies such as local councils or regional authorities.

The truth of the matter was that the proposed assembly represented an unsatisfactory and impracticable halfway house in a unitary state which would be doomed to failure. Clearly, if the United Kingdom is to remain in existence Scottish and Welsh voters must continue to be represented at Westminster. I predicted there would be formidable and often farcical problems that I will raise later in this chapter. If drastic changes were called for – and I did not believe that they were – then the establishment of Scottish and Welsh assemblies must have one of two different results: either Britain would become a federal state, with a written Constitution setting out the powers and scope of the assemblies and Parliament, as the Liberals suggested, or – and this was the long-term aim of the SNP and Plaid Cymru – the United Kingdom would be dismantled, Scottish and Welsh voters would no longer represented at Westminster and Scotland and Wales would take their places as full independent nations. I could not, and still cannot, think of any realistic third alternative without venturing into the realm of fantasy.

But why, it may reasonably be asked, should Britain not become a federal state? After all, West Germany – whose post-war economic record is so enviable by British standards – is a federal state. And why should Britain not have a written

Constitution, in common with the United States and most West European countries?

The German politician Hans Edgar Jahn was a leading member of Chancellor Adenauer's team in the late 1940s and 1950s when the system of the federal republics was being set up by the British and the Americans in the aftermath of the Second World War. He told me that, at that time, the motive of the occupying powers was to hinder the resurgence of a powerful unitary military state in Germany. But he claimed that Adenauer and his entourage realised at a very early stage that decentralisation was likely to make West Germany more and not less efficient. During the war, the Germans experienced the inefficiency of centralised Berlin government; a quarter of a century later, few people would care to deny that the federal system of government has been one of the main factors contributing to the West German economic miracle. So why not transpose it to Britain?

In general terms, one should always be cautious about the feasibility of transplanting a system which has worked well in one country into the different conditions of another. But, more specifically, the German system is fundamentally different from a British scenario in which only Scotland and Wales would be comparable federal states. To pursue the German analogy, it is as if Schleswig-Holstein and Baden-Württemberg were alone to have their own subordinate state legislatures, while at the same time being over-represented in a Bonn parliament which was responsible for the government of the rest of the federal republic. This would be intolerable to other Germans, particularly if the Schleswig-Holstein and Baden-Württemberg representatives determined the complexion of the government in Bonn and were able to deal with matters for which they were not responsible in their own provinces.

Second, the German states are, for the main part, ancient kingdoms, like Bavaria, the Margraviate of Baden or the Hansa cities, with a proud separate history. Only Nordrhein-Westfalen is an artificial new land. The Scottish and the Welsh situations are perhaps broadly comparable but the English position is not. Because England is so much more heavily populated than Scotland or Wales, the federation would be completely out of balance and there were no identifiable demands for subordinate parliaments in Norwich for East Anglia, Winchester for Wessex, Birmingham for Mercia, Manchester for Lancastria or Newcastle for Northumbria – all areas which, in terms of population, are comparable with Scotland or Wales. Bavaria and Niedersachsen are larger than the other German states but their populations are not out of balance. But a federation in which the English made up 83 per cent of the population, the Scots 11 per cent, the Welsh 4 per cent and the Northern Irish 2 per cent I considered just not workable and don't know of the existence of any such working situation.

In 1977, there was no demand for the dismemberment of England itself nor is there any likelihood of such a demand materialising. This is very different from saying that there is no demand for decentralisation. There is – and, in the final chapter, I shall deal with the virtues of decentralisation which do not involve the creation of legislative assemblies and bringing government closer to the people via city regions and traditional counties.

The *sine qua non* of a federal system is a written Constitution. In the absence of a written Constitution and a Supreme Court, which would interpret such a constitution, a federal state would find itself enmeshed in interminable internal difficulties and disputes as to the frontiers of power. Now there is no reason Britain should not, in theory, have a written Constitution. In practice, it would mean altering our way of government far beyond the confines of the Scotland and Wales Bill. And, even if such a radical change were to take place – for which there is little obvious demand in England – would it really solve the problem of Scotland and Wales? The SNP demands nation status, with all the trappings of a separate army, navy, air force and diplomatic representation which accompany nation status. Exactly the same factors which would help to make any devolution settlement unstable would operate in the case of a federal solution. For a federal solution to work, there would have to be a unanimous desire to want to make it work. And it is this that was manifestly lacking in the Scotland of the 1970s.

Allow me a personal reflection and a slight digression. Politicians who claim greater wisdom than their colleagues can find that they are very vulnerable. So, was I generally wiser than my colleagues? No. Did I realise something that they failed to identify and I had done since 1962? Yes. It was a crucial fact of life. It was this. Those men and women who were at the core of the Scottish National Party were simply not interested in a consensual approach. It was in their DNA that they were hell bent on going down in history as the creators of an independent Scottish state. Nothing less. I viewed them not as enemies but as people who held profoundly mistaken beliefs.

Nor was it possible to pretend – as so many politicians would understandably like to – that an assembly in Edinburgh would be little more than a glorified county council and that

its establishment would not alarm anyone on either side of
the border. (All too often one gets the impression that
politicians who favour devolution hope to persuade an
apathetic English electorate that devolution represents little
more than tinkering with Welsh and Scottish local
government and therefore need be of no concern to them
whereas, as we shall see, its implications are enormous – not
only for Scotland and Wales but for the United Kingdom
as a whole.) An elected assembly with legislative power is
neither more nor less than a parliament – it is not a local
authority. Local authorities, whatever their size, have no
power to make or alter the laws they apply – they take
decisions at a purely administrative level within the limits
laid down by the law which is not made by them but by
Parliament. Nor do local authorities attract the feelings of
patriotism and emotion invested in a parliament which acts
as a focus of national pride. An assembly of the kind
then proposed for Edinburgh, whatever the limitations on
its power and whatever its innate implausibility, was a
very different kettle of fish from even the grandest local
authority. It is both misleading and unrealistic to pretend
otherwise.

Given that the assembly is – for all its limitations – an
altogether different political animal from a local authority,
how could it, I thought, function effectively in a unitary state
in which the Westminster Parliament remained the supreme
legislative authority? The answer is that it could not possibly
do so and that conflict, bitterness and resentment could only
follow its establishment. And the fact that so much store had
been set on the proposed assembly by devolutionists would
only have exacerbated these feelings. Expectations which
have been raised and are then thwarted are the stuff of life of

those who have claimed, and continue to claim, that the best solution is for Scotland to make a clean break with its history of the last 300 years.

8

Prescient Cunningham

GEORGE CUNNINGHAM AND I had been ever-present in the chamber during the passage of the Scotland Bill and, the day before the House went in to the 1977 Christmas recess, I gave him my assessment of how things stood: 'It has become obvious that this is a badly drafted and deeply flawed bill. Even the parliamentary draughtsmen have thrown up their hands in horror, saying, "This is the best we can do." The only reason that Ted Short and Michael Foot[1] can give us for proceeding is that there is an overwhelming demand for it in Scotland. We are surely entitled to test whether there is such an "overwhelming" demand.' George agreed and we decided we would put down an amendment establishing a threshold – no matter how much such a move might annoy our Labour colleagues. And they were mightily annoyed. A combination of Labour backbenchers opposed to devolution and the Official Opposition forced through the amendment by 168 votes to 142 votes. The Scotland Act 1978 therefore included the following clause (clause 85):

---

1   In October 1976, Foot had replaced Short as Leader of the House of Commons.

(1) Before a draft of the first order to be made under section 83 of this Act is laid before Parliament a referendum shall be held in accordance with Schedule 17 to this Act on the question whether effect is to be given to the provisions of this Act.

(2) If it appears to the Secretary of State that less than 40 per cent of the persons entitled to vote in the referendum have voted 'Yes' in reply to the question posed in the Appendix to Schedule 17 to this Act or that a majority of the answers given in the referendum have been 'No' he shall lay before Parliament the draft of an Order in Council for the repeal of this Act.

(3) If a draft laid before Parliament under this section is approved by a resolution of each House, Her Majesty in Council may make an Order in the terms of the draft.

Because the threshold was not met in the referendum, the act was repealed.

As it was to mean the difference between having a Scottish assembly/parliament – the distinction was blurred – in 1979 and having a parliament in 1999, I reproduce a significant chunk of Cunningham's contribution to the parliamentary debate concerning the amendment, which took place on 25 January 1978. It shows just how skilfully Cunningham dealt with the contentions of pro-devolution MPs, eager to pick holes in our arguments.

Mr George Cunningham (Labour, Islington South and Finsbury): I beg to move my Amendment (a).

The hon. Member for North Angus and Mearns [Alick Buchanan-Smith] declared his opposition to the whole idea of holding referendums, and he questioned whether this was a desirable practice or one which took away from the powers of Parliament. Surely, the criteria appropriate to deciding whether one should have a referendum on any subject are pretty clear. It is desirable to hold a referendum on any major constitutional matter on which the opinion of the electorate cannot be gathered from the way in which the electorate voted in a General Election. That will normally be the situation where there is a division of opinion or a major division of opinion within the main political parties.

There is no way in which one could have decided what the people of Britain wanted on membership of the Community, for example, by reference to how they voted in a General Election. Some Labour candidates were for membership of the Community and some were against. The same was the case within the Conservative Party.

Precisely the same situation exists with regard to devolution, on which there is a division of opinion within the parties. Therefore the only way in which we can tell what the electorate wants on this issue, as on membership of the European Economic Community, is to test it directly, otherwise one is forced to realign the parties in accordance with the division of opinion on the issue one wants to test, and that, of course, is not a practical possibility.

Cunningham went on to say that he wanted to know what his bosses, the electorate, thought:

Whether I then follow that is for me, the Member, to decide, taking into account that they are acting as the major factor. But there are also other considerations as well, including the Member's own conscience, that being one of the factors involved, but only one of the factors involved . . .

The reasons why, in my opinion, it is right [to have a referendum] can be quickly stated. First, it is a major constitutional change. Second, it is one on which the parties are divided within themselves. The division of opinion on the subject is not consistent with the division between the political parties. Third, it is in practice an irrevocable step. No one knows that more than the SNP. The SNP knows that, though this Parliament could tear up the devolution Bill after it had been brought into force, that is not a matter of practical politics.

Then we have the fact that we all know that, if devolution goes ahead, we shall all, to put it at its most modest, have to cross our fingers and hope (a) that it does not lead to constant haggles between Edinburgh and London, as many of us think it will, and (b) that those haggles will not lead to a progression towards independence without the people of Scotland wanting independence but always feeling that they can achieve a more logical arrangement by taking one further step and then one further step. Those are the considerations that make me feel that there should be a referendum on this issue.

How prescient Cunningham was!

Then there is the question of what kind of minimum test we need to impose. There is, of course, a minimum test implicit in having a referendum at all – namely, that more people should vote 'Yes' than should vote 'No'. The only question is whether we impose a minimum majority.

There are two ways in which to do that. First, we could require a minimum percentage of the electorate to vote, however they voted, and, secondly, we could require a minimum majority of those who vote 'Yes' over those who vote 'No' . . .

My hon. Friend the Member for Mitcham and Morden [Bruce Douglas-Mann] suggests 33⅓ per cent; I suggest 40 per cent. We should all recognise that there is nothing magic or sacred about any figure in this context. If there were any very natural figure to be found, it would be 50 per cent. One might say that, on a matter of this importance and of this irrevocable nature, we should require that 50 per cent of the electorate should vote for it or we do not go ahead. But no one is proposing that. We could have gone for a more modest proposal – that 45 per cent of the electorate should vote for it. We are not going for that. I am suggesting a very modest figure – that 40 per cent of the electorate in Scotland should declare positive support for the proposal, or the referendum does not bind us morally to go ahead with devolution.

I do not think that that can be called a wrecking amendment for devolution, first because it is not a figure which was not met in the EEC referendum. The EEC figure for the whole of the United Kingdom was that just under 43 per cent voted 'Yes'. That is, 43 per cent of the electorate in the United Kingdom as a whole voted 'Yes'. Therefore, my test, if imposed in the referendum, would have been very comfortably met.

Secondly, if the Government are right, if the SNP is right and if the hon. Member for South Ayrshire [Jim Sillars] for the Scottish Labour Party is right – that the people of Scotland overwhelmingly want devolution – there is no problem. If they overwhelmingly want devolution, far more than 40 per cent will presumably vote for it. I am not asking that the overwhelming majority, or even that the majority, should vote for it, but only that 40 per cent should be prepared to go out and vote for it . . .

Let us look at the kind of polls which are achieved in Scotland. Let us not take just the last year or two but look back over a prolonged period of time and take the figures for the last quarter of the century, omitting 1945 because that was unusual at the end of the war and there was an out-of-date register. Over the nine General Elections, the average poll in Scotland was 77.4 per cent. If that were the poll in the devolution referendum, my test would require that the 'Yeses' should get 51 per cent of those who actually vote. Only 51.7 per cent is a very, very modest margin above a fair majority.

The lower the poll, the larger the majority needs to be. That is in the nature of things. If the poll were 70 per cent, the 'Yeses' would need to obtain 57 per cent of the votes cast. If the poll were 65 per cent – and surely it cannot be as low as that if the overwhelming majority of the Scottish people want devolution – the 'Yeses' would have to get 57.5 per cent of the votes cast. I hope that no one is proposing to impose devolution if the poll is actually less than 65 per cent.

If the poll were only 60 per cent and 40 per cent of the Scottish people cared so much about devolution that they stayed at home, it would be necessary to obtain two-thirds of the votes cast. Some would believe that that was perfectly natural for a constitutional change such as this.

I quote these statistics to show that if there is anything like a reasonable poll, if there is anything like a normal poll in Scotland, even my test is one which requires the 'Yeses' to exceed the 'Noes' by a tiny margin, by not much more than 50 per cent, which any threshold would require.

The SNP has been telling us for a long time that the people of Scotland over the last quarter of a century have not really had the full range of choice before them. After all, in most of the elections most electors have had what the SNP would regard as a poor choice—between the Labour, Liberal and Conservative Parties. They have not had the SNP. Nevertheless, they have voted on average to the tune of 77.4 per cent. If they did that with their restricted choice, we must assume that, faced with devolution—which we are told they are dying to have—they will surely come out in these numbers at least.

Mr Gordon Wilson (Dundee East, SNP):
The hon. Member has said that we say that the Scottish people are dying to have devolution. I do not know where he has been. Perhaps he has been in Islington all his life. What the SNP has been saying is that the Scottish people should have control over their own affairs. They are being offered devolution by the Government, but not the choice that we want.

Mr Cunningham:

We all know that the SNP will try to get its supporters to vote for devolution, not because it believes in devolution – the SNP at least is perfectly honest about this – but because it wants its supporters to vote 'Yes' in the referendum because it knows – it is honest enough to admit it – that getting devolution is not only the easiest way of getting independence but is the only way in which they stand a cat in hell's chance of getting independence.

Those who want independence will be voting 'Yes' and those who genuinely want devolution – although they are limited in number – will also vote 'Yes'. They are faced with that choice – not a choice of individuals but a choice of a system of government which, we are told, they want either in its own right or as a paving stone to independence. If the people do not come out at least in their normal proportions, that will tell us something and we are entitled to take that into account and say that a majority is required of the 'Yeses' over the 'Noes'.

This referendum will not be mandatory. Nothing will be legally binding upon the House of Commons. Whatever comes before the House in the way of an order from the Government will be passed or not passed according to the discretion of the House. Anyone who feels that a referendum is all right if it is not binding should not be worried about my amendment, because these changes would have no effect upon that point.

Equally, the failing of the test does not mean that devolution does not go ahead. I want to stress that strongly. Let us assume that only 37 per cent, or whatever the figure is, votes 'Yes' in the referendum. That does not mean that devolution necessarily stops. All it means is that the Minister has to produce an order which has the form of repealing the Act and to put that order before the House. It would then be entirely up to the House whether to pass it. I can certainly foresee circumstances in which, because the test had not been met but had nearly been met and the number of 'Noes' was particularly low, the House would decide that in all the circumstances it would not repeal, although the matter had been brought to the House to consider repeal.

Mr Gordon Wilson:

The hon. Member proposes to lay down certain minima for the votes in the referendum and then says that, if the vote falls just short of the standard he has set, the House would still have a discretion and would be acting on an order which had an impact. Does the hon. Member accept that those who can best gauge the opinion of the Scottish people are the Scottish Members of Parliament and that only they should have the right to vote on such a motion?

Mr Cunningham:

I take the view that only the Scottish people, in the way defined by the SNP, are entitled to decide whether Scotland becomes independent. The question is whether Scotland should become independent. Only the Scottish people, as defined by the SNP, are entitled to take that decision, and not English Members or English Members with Scottish accents.

But that does not apply to devolution, because devolution does not affect only Scotland. It affects the whole of the United Kingdom. If it is a half-and-half thing which messes up our system, we are entitled to have a say in it. If we did not, the cry would soon go up 'You have got votes in our Parliament and we have not got votes in your.' That entitles the English to have a say in the matter.

The only effect of this threshold is that, if the threshold is not met, the House has to reconsider the matter; the Government would have to bring in an order which requires the House of Commons to reconsider the matter. It does not seek to terminate devolution automatically, and in practice it would not necessarily do so. It simply imposes a level and provides that if that level is not reached the House of Commons will want to look at the matter again. In my view, it would not be fair to hold a referendum without giving any indication to the Scottish people that we propose to take account of the size of the poll and of the size of the majority, both of which are involved in this type of amendment.

The test is a reasonable one for such a fundamental and irrevocable change as is being proposed. The figure is even perhaps a shade too modest. If the SNP and the Government are even remotely right in saying that a significant majority of Scottish people want this change, they have nothing to worry about. Yet we are observing that they are worried. The Scottish Labour Party is to vote against my amendment, and the hon. Member for South Ayrshire will no doubt make his own points.

The SNP, which says that Scotland wants this change, is against the amendment, and so are the Government. The only people who should be against it are those who, whether they say so or not, suspect that there is not a majority of people in Scotland positively in favour of the amendment but who are determined to impose it whether that majority exists or not. If they believe in what they have been told about opinion in Scotland, they have absolutely nothing to fear from my amendment.

9

'I Have Bequeathed to You the West Lothian Question'

❖

THROUGHOUT 1978, UNTIL they received royal assent at the end of July, the Scotland and Wales Bills meandered their weary ways through the House of Commons. The attitudes of my colleagues in the Parliamentary Labour Party were varied. There were some, true believers in devolution, who were livid because they rightly foresaw that, if passed, it would scupper the entire devolution project. Dennis Canavan was one of the true believers and, a quarter of a century later, he would become the chairman of the Yes Advisory Board of Yes Scotland in the 2014 Referendum. There were others who did not understand what all the fuss was about and were frustrated that there was little or no parliamentary time for the issues that concerned them. I understood and sympathised. Then there was Michael Foot, nominally in charge of the legislation. Part of him was exasperated but part of him, the great parliamentarian that he was, thought that the House of Commons must have its say – after all, he had been no less difficult as a backbencher over Vietnam and European legislation.

And then there was the prime minister, himself. Any time I saw him in the corridors of the Commons in 1978, he hardly ever failed to give me a cheerful wink, which I interpreted as meaning he knew what George Cunningham and I were up to. It probably suited him that we were chuntering on and on while he was trying to put the economy in a more favourable position. But he wasn't going to say anything openly to us in case it landed him in trouble with Michael Foot and risked antagonising the 12 SNP MPs he needed to keep on board to sustain the government's majority. These were circumstances that afforded me being shown tolerance rather than the wrath of party discipline.

On every clause and subclause, I would regurgitate the same question, 'How could I vote on the issue under discussion, as it affected Blackburn Lancashire, but, under the terms of the bill, could not vote on the same issue as it affected Blackburn, West Lothian?' And, whenever the young whip, Peter Snape, who represented West Bromwich, was on Whip's duty, on the frontbench, I would amend it to: 'How can I vote on matters in relation to West Bromwich, but will be unable to do so on the very same relation to West Lothian?' A whip is forever silent but Peter Snape told me that he had repeated the question to the Chief Whip, Michael Cocks, and asked, 'What's the bloody answer?' to which Cocks gave the helpful reply, 'Fuck me if I know!'

A few days later, when Cocks was in the chamber, it occurred to me to enquire, 'How is it that I will be able to vote on all matters of education in Bristol[1] but not on any matter of education in Bathgate, Blackburn, Blackridge, Bo'ness and Broxburn in my own West Lothian constituency?'

---

1   Cocks's home city and constituency.

The Chief Whip raised his eyes to the ceiling of the chamber, as if to indicate his true feeling and implying, 'What are the Labour government doing putting forward such a ridiculous piece of legislation?'

When I repeated the question of Scots MPs being able to vote on English matters but English MPs not being able to vote on the very same matters pertaining to Scotland for the hundredth-plus time, I intoned it rather pompously, adding, 'It cannot be asked too often.' John Smith turned round from the frontbench and snapped at me, 'Oh, yes, Tam, it bloody well can!' Whereupon Enoch Powell gravely rose in his place and said that the House had 'finally grasped' what the Honourable Gentlemen for West Lothian is on about. 'Let us,' Powell suggested, 'give it the soubriquet of the West Lothian question in order to save time.' – though saving time, of course, was the last thing he wanted to do.

When I went to see Enoch, 11 days before he died, he said in a hoarse whisper – he had cancer of the throat – 'I have bequeathed to you the West Lothian question.' – and so he had. Like all politicians, I am a man of a certain vanity – but not nearly sufficient vanity as to call a constitutional conundrum after myself!

Another conundrum which had a significant bearing on the devolution debate at the time and all subsequent discussion of the matter was the Barnett formula – the mechanism by which the Treasury dictates the level of public spending in Scotland, Northern Ireland and Wales. Lord Joel Barnett had originally come up with this controversial Whitehall formula. Allow me to be personal. The late Joel Barnett, a clever, charming, Jewish accountant from Manchester, was my parliamentary colleague for 40 years and my friend for half a century until he died in 2014. In the years that he was Chief Secretary to the Treasury (1974–79), after late-night votes in the Commons and having told his government driver to go home in the early evening, we would walk back to the Horseferry Road, as our London flats were near one another. He would reiterate that what he was doing for Scotland – he eschewed the word 'formula' – was less generous than its predecessor, the Goschen formula, that had operated from the 1880s.[2] Barnett accepted that the Union had been partly about the transfer of resources from richer to poorer areas and that there had been few complaints about this throughout the 20th century.

A Manchester United season ticket holder, he would observe wryly that he knew all about Aberdeen and North Sea oil from his friend (later Sir) Alex Ferguson. But it was

---

2   In simple terms, the Goschen formula, like the Barnett formula, was used to calculate the relative spend per capita of public money based on the ratio of the population of Scotland (and Ireland) to that of England and Wales. When it was introduced in 1888, the ratio for England and Wales to Scotland was calculated to be 80:11 (for Ireland, prior to 1922 and the creation of the Irish Free State, it was 80:9). This was the fixed proportion and, over the years until the Barnett formula was introduced in 1978, it took no account of the fact that the population in England grew quite significantly more than Scotland's which, of course, benefitted Scotland. After the end of the Second World War, the Secretaries of State for Scotland had successfully argued that no downward negotiations of the formula should be allowed because of Scotland's various special circumstances – the remoteness of some parts of the country, the number of very sparsely populated areas, chronic poverty and, in the Central Belt, overcrowded and insanitary housing – all of which called for extra funding not less.

his own view that the windfall of oil reserves had blinded people to the fact that we have returned to a position whereby the basic fabric of Scotland was held together by these transfers. Barnett displayed a tinge of uncharacteristic irritation when he was confronted by the argument of Gordon Wilson, MP for Dundee, that continuing relative poverty was a reason for secession when he realised that breaking up the Union would only make things worse. As Barnett saw it, the higher cost of public services is the natural, inescapable consequence of a country occupying half the land area of the rest of the United Kingdom and with one tenth of the population. From his accountant's perspective, Scotland was quite simply more expensive to run. Barnett's qualms chimed with my belief that Scotland is better considered on a regional basis. Dryly, he observed on one occasion, 'Just you remember that Edinburgh Morningside is a good deal better-heeled than Manchester Gorton and the people in St Andrews are more comfortably off than people in St Helens.'

Barnett was a champion of a concept that has now become a reality – a powerhouse centred on Greater Manchester. Nonetheless, he could not hide his resentment – and nor could I – of the SNP's perpetual antagonism towards London. All Unionist parties accepted that everyone in Britain benefits from the extraordinary wealth and revenues of one of the world's great cities and economic powerhouses. Where was the reciprocal generosity of spirit in the nationalist view that 'it's oor oil and we'll keep it'?

As a nonagenarian, he told me that, although he was a passionate supporter of the United Kingdom, the one big personal gain for him, if the 'Yes' vote had won in the 2014 independence referendum, was that it would have killed off the formula which bears his name. In 1978 when he devised the formula, Barnett was Chief Secretary to the Treasury – the third most important man in the Cabinet, after James Callaghan and the chancellor, Denis Healey. Former ministers usually parade their political legacy and defend it to their utmost. So why should my friend and colleague say he would have been pleased if the formula had been scrapped? Barnett said the formula is 'fundamentally flawed' since it 'wildly' overestimates Scotland's population and therefore gives the Scots a disproportionate slice of UK tax revenues. Here we have its inventor damning his creation while, fast-forward 36 years, all three party leaders, in the wake of the 'No' vote in the 2014 referendum, were lining up to extol the Barnett formula as a central plank in their 'devo-max' settlement for Scotland.

Barnett also reminded me that he was the first to give evidence to a House of Lords Select Committee in 2008 on the Barnett formula. Actually, this committee did a great deal of research and reported that Scotland at that time got £1,600 more per head per year than England in public expenditure. It is this that has meant that Scotland has been able to cap and then scrap prescription charges, provide free care for the elderly and sustain Scottish students having their university tuition fees paid for them – objectives that English taxpayers would surely like but can't have. SNP propaganda that the Barnett formula benefits the English to the disadvantage of the Scots is just not true.

When I last talked to him on the phone, he reiterated what he has said many times before: 'As Chief Secretary, you remember I was having a terrible time doing what I didn't go into politics to do – cutting public expenditure. And I was having meetings with every departmental minister about their budgets. They all wanted more money – Tony Benn and

Barbara Castle more than most. I decided I could placate at least three Cabinet ministers – the Secretaries of State for Scotland, Wales and Northern Ireland – if I could settle on a formula for their budgets. So I set up this method of allocating public expenditure that the Labour Cabinet then agreed to.' Barnett told me that he himself never called it a 'formula'. That only came later when Margaret Thatcher and John Major carried on with it. What Lord Barnett had known but did not challenge in the heat of the moment, during the 1976 IMF bailout of Britain and the 1978–79 Winter of Discontent, was the starting point of the arrangement – the estimate of Scotland's population which was plain wrong. He told me he suspected that the figures were significantly out of date but that he was desperate to get a system which would save the Treasury trouble. The reason that the Barnett formula has lasted so long is that it saves people trouble and it saves prime ministers from having rows.

Before the 1979 referendum, the last thing the Labour Cabinet wanted was to be seen to be clawing back money from Scottish voters.

In contrast to 2014, the 1979 referendum campaign was a meek affair. Most Labour and Conservative MPs sat mute on the fence. The official policy of the Labour Party was to vote 'Yes' and only zealots for devolution objected to Labour's 'Vote No' campaign which was led by Brian Wilson, with me as vice chairman and the great letter-writer to the papers, Archie Birt, a party activist from Gourock, as secretary. The position was encapsulated when George Foulkes, then a talkative member of the executive of the Labour Party in

Scotland, suggested to Jimmy Allison, organiser of the Scottish Labour Party, that I should be disciplined for not toeing the party line. Allison replied that it would be a bit difficult to do that as he hadn't even been able to persuade his own mother and wife, both of whom were Labour stalwarts and former provosts of Paisley, to vote 'Yes'.

Jim Sillars and I toured Scotland in the run-up to the 1979 referendum, putting the case for (him) and against (me) devolution. In total we had 18 encounters and we even went in midwinter to such remote places as Mallaig. The one point Sillars and I did agree on was that devolution would inevitably lead to something that was indistinguishable from a separate state. After 37 years, Sillars – still a personal friend – and I, have been proved right. The only difference is that he wanted it and I, just as emphatically, did not. Both Sillars and I recognised that, if the Scots decisively voted for an independent, separate Scottish state, then so be it. Where we differed related to my view that, if there were to be any form of devolution, then the English would be affected and were, therefore, entitled to a say.

During those journeys round Scotland, it became clear to me that, generally, support for devolution was lukewarm, with the strongest pro-devolutionary sentiments expressed in the fishing communities of the north-east – an area which was to vote decisively 'No' in the 2014 referendum.

An ever-present thorn in the flesh of the enthusiasts for a Scottish parliament has been the position of the islanders and, in particular, the Shetlanders who point out that their nearest railway station is in Bergen, Norway. The difference between the 'Island communities' and the rest of Scotland was later to be fully recognised when the Scottish Constitutional Convention opined that 'there is agreement that the unique place of the Islands warrants separate constitutional consideration in the detailed legislative proposals for the establishment of Scotland's Parliament and the range of powers and responsibilities'.[3]

In the autumn of 1978, I had gone on a campaigning visit to Shetland for the Labour 'Vote No' campaign. At one meeting, the patriarchal convener Alexander Tulloch, chairman of the Shetland Islands Council, said in his soft Shetland drawl, 'I run a business making the highest quality rugs, shawls, dressing gowns and sweaters, giving work to many people throughout the Islands. How would a talking-shop in Edinburgh help business or the Shetland County Council? We would be better to remain with the devil we know in London. Or, if that is not possible, we might be better off with Oslo.' Others thought that the SNP slogan, 'It's our oil', might be translated as 'It's Shetland's oil'. There was a widespread consensus that the islands – Orkney, Shetland and the Hebrides – were a case apart. When the votes were counted, it was clear that Shetland had emphatically voted 'No' by a margin of almost four to one. In fact, the Shetland 'No' vote was the highest in the country.

During the lead-up to the referendum, Jim Callaghan got

---

3 *Scottish Government Yearbook 1992*, pp 93–4. The Scottish Constitutional Convention evolved from the cross-party Campaign for a Scottish Assembly (CSA). After the 1979 referendum failed to deliver sufficient votes for the legislation to be enacted, those in favour of devolution kept their hopes for a Scottish assembly alive through the CSA which was formed in 1980. At the helm was the respected political scientist Jack Brand. He was succeeded by the Labour Party's Jim Boyack, the father of former Labour MSP Sarah Boyack who lost her Edinburgh Central seat to the Scottish Conservative leader Ruth Davidson in the 2016 Scottish parliamentary elections.

really angry with me for the first time in his premiership. In February 1979, Brian Wilson, Archie Birt and I, the leaders of the Labour 'Vote No' campaign, took a case against the Independent Television Authority to the Court of Session in Edinburgh over the issue of whether ITV was giving our side of the campaign a fair hearing. Lord Ross, then a senior judge and later Lord Justice Clerk, found in our favour. Callaghan thought it was an outrage to use the court to torpedo the Party's official support for ITV's arrangements.

The result of the referendum on 1 March 1979 was a narrow win for the Yes camp (51.6 per cent as opposed to a 'No' vote of 48.4 per cent). But the figures fell far short of the conditions imposed by George Cunningham's amendment of February 1978 for a threshold. And, in Wales, the result was a decisive 'No', with just 20 per cent of those who voted in favour of a Welsh assembly.

Incandescent with rage, the Scottish Nationalists MPs voted against the Labour government in a motion brought by the Leader of the Opposition, Margaret Thatcher, that 'this House has no confidence in Her Majesty's Government'. James Callaghan took the government's case to the country and a general election was held on 3 May 1979. As in 1945, there had been seismic changes of mood in British politics, Mrs Thatcher entered Downing Street and the SNP MPs, who had been warned that, by bringing the Labour government down, they were like 'turkeys voting for an early Christmas', were reduced to just two. After a decent period, Callaghan resigned as Leader of the Opposition in November 1980 and Michael Foot was elected in his place.

As for me, in the autumn of 1978, concerned that I would lose the West Lothian seat, the Labour Party organised an opinion poll in the constituency which, they said, gave them cause for alarm on account of my ferocious anti-devolution views. As it turned out, my 2,000-plus majority in the second election of 1974 soared to over 20,000 in May 1979 – the largest majority in Scotland. Combined with what was close to a parliamentary obliteration of the SNP, my own result led me to think, 'Well, that's put the SNP's gas on a peep forever. That's that.' How wrong I was to be proved over the next 35 years.

10

Devolution Pushed on to the Back Burner

❖

To UNDERSTAND THE train of events which ensued after the collapse of the Scotland and Wales Bills in March 1979, it is necessary to consider the background and character of Donald Dewar, the man who, perhaps more than anyone, was the driving force for devolution in the 1980s. But, before doing so, it is better to be candid. From the time he was re-elected to the House of Commons as MP for Glasgow Garscadden in April 1978, Dewar did not like me and I, slowly over the years until he died, had an increasing distaste for him. I was one of Dewar's outcasts. So was George Galloway. So was Dennis Canavan, in particular, partly because Dewar never forgave Canavan for defeating him at the selection conference in West Stirlingshire, to succeed Willie Baxter, the farmer and hotel owner, in 1974. A number of good colleagues in the Scottish Labour group were also 'excluded' and, to me, any serious political discussion seemed to only take place between Dewar and his parliamentary acolytes. In my experience, most politicians are charitable towards those who hold different views from their own but I never found this to be the case with Dewar who tended to ignore or dismiss the views of colleagues who were not of his persuasion.

Donald Campbell Dewar, the only child of Alisdair Dewar, a well-respected Glasgow GP and dermatologist, spent a 'lonely childhood' – his own description – but, after attending Glasgow Academy, he blossomed at Glasgow University. He joined the university's debating group, the Glasgow University Dialectic Society, which became well known for winning the *Observer* Mace more than any other UK university. Having qualified as a solicitor in 1963, the following year he married the talented and beautiful Alison McNair and the couple had a son and a daughter. Unexpectedly, he beat the sitting Conservative MP, Lady Tweedsmuir, in Aberdeen South in 1966. Because he had come through to West Lothian to canvass for me at my by-election in 1962, I went up to Aberdeen to speak with him at a meeting and go round the doors. Having done so, I was in a position to know that he was an excellent young candidate but, at that time, there was not a trace of Donald Dewar playing any particularly Scottish card. My memory is that he was full of praise, justifiably, for the work of Labour councillors, not least Jimmy Lamond, later Lord Provost of Aberdeen and MP for Oldham East, who was to be a stalwart anti-devolutionist. Equally, I am absolutely certain that there was no inkling of Dewar wanting a Scottish assembly when he succeeded Christopher Price (MP Birmingham Perry Barr) as Tony Crosland's PPS, at the Board of Trade in 1967. At the time, I was Dick Crossman's PPS and had a lot to do with Donald Dewar.

Given the national swing towards Edward Heath, it wasn't too surprising when Dewar lost his seat to the Conservative Iain Sproat at the 1970 general election and had to return to Scotland to earn his living with the legal firm of Ross Harper and Murphy and as a highly respected solicitor on children's panels.

At weekends, Dewar came to my home on a number of occasions for a meal. My wife and I sadly observed that he was becoming ever more morose and dejected. We thought at first this was because he had not been considered for the shortlist of candidates for several Scottish seats – local CLPs, at that time, had a certain animosity towards ex-MPs of the 1966–70 parliament – but the root of his despondency may well have been the break-up of his marriage and the agony of seeing his son and daughter being brought up in another man's house – it must have been all the more difficult for Dewar to take when that other man was Derry Irvine, who was to become his fellow Cabinet member and Tony Blair's Lord Chancellor. This was a scar which was to have huge political consequence.

Dewar came to resent London and became passionate about bringing power to Scotland. Almost single-handedly in the Labour Party, he kept the devolutionary flame burning. As we have seen, John Smith never gave devolution another public thought. Bruce Millan, the Secretary of State for Scotland until 1979 and Shadow Secretary of State until 1983, was annoyed with me on grounds of what he deemed to be party disloyalty for my well-known antipathy towards devolution. However, none of us ever did detect Millan's real feelings about devolution and he went to Brussels where he was an effective and successful European Commissioner for Regional Policy. Harry Ewing, a junior minister in the Scottish Office and the joint chairman with David Steel of the Scottish Constitutional Convention, began to get cheesed off with travelling to London and, following his resignation in 1992 after Labour lost the general election, was made a life peer. Ewing had long been a member of the Constitutional Convention and when he took up his position in the House of Lords as Baron Ewing of Kirkford, he became a front-bench spokesman on Scottish affairs. He resigned from both roles in 1996. In 1980, Michael Foot became Labour Party Leader after Callaghan's resignation, a position he held for almost three years. Considering I had been instrumental in torpedoing referendum legislation he had been responsible for, he was the most generous of men when he appointed me to the frontbench as his science spokesman for the Opposition. And, truth to tell, to my discredit, having got a majority of over 20,000 in May 1979, I forgot about the devolution issue for those three years. Dewar, meanwhile, was Chairman of the Select Committee on Scottish Affairs from 1979 to 1981. From this position, he gradually continued to shift the devolution issue back on to the political agenda. In this, he was hugely helped by economic and political circumstances.

It is my considered opinion that, had Willie Whitelaw become Tory leader and prime minister, the devolution issue would have been, as many of us assumed it would be, put to bed. Whitelaw had been a decorated officer in the Scots Guards during the Second World War and was happily married to Celia Sprot, a member of the well-respected Sprot family of Haystoun. He had cut his political teeth in contesting the unwinnable seat of East Dunbartonshire in 1950 and 1951 and he certainly would not have grated on the Scots or raised our hackles in the way that Mrs Thatcher was to do. Nor do I think for one moment that Whitelaw would have sanctioned his chancellor, were it Geoffrey Howe or anyone else, to bring in the draconian budgets of the early 1980s that did so much damage to traditional industries in Scotland and those who worked in them. But, leaving the realm of what might have been aside, the actuality was an unsolicited gift to Dewar and those who thought like him. He nurtured the feeling that the assembly the Scots never got would have protected us from the ravages of Mrs Thatcher. Nothing of the kind would have happened because the assembly, as it had been proposed in 1979, could have done precious little, if anything at all, to protect Scotland from Mrs Thatcher's dogmas. The argument is irrelevant as such an assembly would not have had the necessary economic powers. Yet many people in Scotland succumbed to the glitz and easy propaganda that, if only we had had the assembly that the wicked Tam Dalyell and George Cunningham deprived us of, all would have been well.

Events have a habit of taking over and there were a number of unforeseen circumstances over the coming years which distracted my mind from devolution. On 2 April 1982, Argentine forces landed on the Falkland Islands. For the next three years, apart from my constituency work, my mind was focused on the circumstances of the naval and military action, on the sinking of the Argentine cruiser *General Belgrano* and on Mrs Thatcher's lying about her knowledge of the Peruvian peace proposals, which had led me to make a 48-hour visit (at my own expense) to see Peru's President Fernando Belaúnde Terry and his prime minister, Manuel Ulloa Elías, who had formulated the peace proposals on his own typewriter and got them to the British prime minister. Meanwhile Dewar was, from 1983, embarking on an 11-year stint on Scottish Affairs on the Opposition frontbench. Step by step, stealthily, he was committing the party to ever more and more devolution.

Scarcely had the dominance of the Falklands War in the news subsided than Britain was convulsed by the miners' strike. In general terms, it dampened the cry for devolution – the theme was solidarity among mining communities in Scotland, England and Wales. But, in one particular respect, a consequence of the miners' strike did enhance the devolutionary cause. Through the various involvements of Mrs Thatcher's controversial advisor David Hart in the coal industry, blacklegs infuriated the law-abiding NUM at Polkemmet, the second largest colliery in Scotland. In anger, the strikers turned off the pumps, flooding the pit to an extent that inevitably led to its closure. Since Polkemmet was the coking coalmine which supplied the huge steel complex at Ravenscraig, the damage done at the West Lothian pit was a major factor which led to the closure of Ravenscraig and the demise of the steel industry in Scotland. This gave oxygen to the devolutionary cause – and I believe the enduring bitterness over Ravenscraig is one of the reasons North Lanarkshire was one of the four areas where the majority of the electorate voted 'Yes' in the 2014 referendum.

It was the view of the late Jeremy Bray, MP for Motherwell South, a man with much experience of the steel industry, that fault also lay with the management of British Steel. Before his tragic death, he told me that the leaders of British Steel, and Sir Robert ('Black Bob') Scholey in particular, were apprehensive about huge investment in Scotland, on account of possible devolutionary developments. This was perhaps the first inkling of a growing attitude in industrial boardrooms to place new investment in England rather than Scotland, in circumstances where there was a balance – just to be safe.

In addition to the Falklands War and the miners' issue, there were other factors that pushed devolution, as far as I was concerned, on to the back burner. In 1985, I was elected to the constituency section of the National Executive Committee (NEC) of the Labour Party – the first Scot to be so for 40 years. Unlike now, this was then a body of real importance. Dewar and those around him were far from pleased. In fact, they were mightily displeased. It was irksome that I had been elected in the first place. It was doubly irksome that I might cause trouble for those calling for a Scottish assembly/ parliament, by going to the trade union leaders I was seeing a lot of during 1985–86 to try to snuff out any reference to devolution in the 1987 Labour manifesto. And they feared (correctly) that Neil Kinnock was, at this time, speaking with a forked tongue on devolution – he had so many other Labour Party troubles and could have been vulnerable to the warnings of people like me. Behind my back, Dewar was at his hurtful snidest, commenting to parliamentary colleagues that I was a 'dotty maverick', not to be taken seriously.

Dennis Canavan, on the other hand, was cheerfully (and comradely, in the best sense) outspoken to my face. Alas, none of them need have bothered. Business on the NEC was dominated entirely by the issue of what to do about the Militant tendency and, in particular, the convulsions of the Liverpool City Labour Party. I voted in favour of expelling Derek Hatton, deputy leader of Liverpool City Council, from the Labour Party because he belonged to Militant. Although he too belonged to Militant, I voted against expelling the prominent Liverpool councillor Tony Mulhearn, and to defend Felicity Dowling on the grounds that Michael Swann, who chaired a government committee set up by Shirley Williams to look in to the education of children from ethnic minority groups, had found Liverpool Education Committee, which Dowling chaired, the best in the country for racial minorities. By taking these decisions, I managed to displease both Kinnock and the far Left. Added to the fact that Ken Livingstone circulated a pamphlet to every constituency Labour Party in the country, asking them if they really wanted me, a pro-European, pro-civil nuclear power, old Etonian on the NEC, it is not surprising that I lost more votes in one year than any other NEC member has done before or since. Then there was the Westland affair – the argument between Michael Heseltine, Secretary of State for Defence, and Leon Brittan, at the department of Trade and Industry, on the purchase of American or European helicopters by the Ministry of Defence. I was the MP who named Colette Bowe (now Dame), on the floor of the House, as the press officer in the Department of Trade and Industry, who had revealed the story of the selectively leaked Law Officer's letter which led to Michael Heseltine storming out of Mrs Thatcher's Cabinet. As a result, I was chucked out of the House three times for claiming that Mrs Thatcher had 'lied' about her involvement in the selective leaking of a law officer's letter – fibbed she had indeed! And I had also spent 11 fraught days at the Old Bailey during the trial of Clive Ponting, the Ministry of Defence civil servant who had sent me a postcard confirming Mrs Thatcher's deceit over the sinking of the *General Belgrano*.

The political atmosphere by the late 1980s had become febrile. Into this combustible hotchpotch was thrown the grenade of the Poll Tax, something that would add more fuel to the devolutionary fire. It has often been described as an evil notion and unfair, as its opponents claimed. A hospital nurse was to pay as much as a Croesus-rich businessman or great landowner. Personally, I don't think, in this context, Mrs Thatcher and those around her were evil – it was more a case of them being exasperated. The rating valuation system throughout the UK had long been seen by all political parties as being in need of an overhaul. The Layfield Committee had met in the House of Commons, Committee Room 14, every Tuesday and Thursday morning, from 10.30 until 1 p.m., when Parliament was sitting, considering local government finance, and had come up with no practical solutions. The 'something must be done syndrome' took over. Result – the Poll Tax. George Younger, the Secretary of State for Scotland, was going bananas about the rates problem in Scotland. By some alchemy, the true nature of which I am far from clear about, the decision was arrived at to try it out in Scotland first. Only two English MPs, both Conservatives – Patrick Cormack, MP for South Staffordshire (now Lord Cormack), and Norman Miscampbell, MP for Blackpool North – had the foresight to vote against their government over the imposition of the Poll Tax in Scotland.

Mayhem was unleashed. People who had never protested in their lives before took to the streets. The politics of grievance exploded as Scots felt that they were being used as guinea pigs.[1] This cacophony of righteous indignation was

---

1   As a Scottish MP in Westminster, it seemed to me that Scotland was being treated unfairly in having the Poll Tax introduced there before the rest of the UK and the Scots had every right to consider themselves as guinea pigs. Some commentators have since said that far from the Poll Tax being foisted on Scotland by a government that didn't give two hoots about those north of the Border, it was done in order to help Scottish businesses that were struggling in the face of having to pay rates that they couldn't afford. If I, an insider, wasn't

grist to the mill of those who supported the Scottish Constitutional Convention and screamed that the assembly that Tam Dalyell, George Cunningham, Brian Wilson and other scoundrels had robbed the Scots of back in 1979 would have protected them from the infamous Poll Tax. That an assembly in Edinburgh as then proposed could have done little of the kind in affording such protection was neither here nor there. They would not have had the levers of economic power to do so. But still the hysteria for a Scottish parliament was rampant.

Margaret Thatcher's imposition of the Poll Tax in Scotland before it became law in the rest of the UK was a catastrophic error. But this was only part of the problem. As Patrick Cormack later wrote to me in March 2015, she was also 'not strong on constitutional issues', adding:

> Margaret Thatcher's biggest failure was North of the Border. She came to power after a referendum which had indicated strong support for devolution – even if not at a level which crossed the threshold Parliament had sensibly imposed. After the '79 election a number of us suggested to her that specific action should be taken to maintain the integrity of the Union. The Scottish Grand Committee[2] should, we recommended, have most of its meetings in Edinburgh and Glasgow, and

---

aware that this was the supposed reason for the early introduction of the Poll Tax in Scotland, how were ordinary Scots supposed to know?

2   The Scottish Grand Committee is a House of Commons committee. All of the members of the Westminster Parliament representing Scottish constituencies are entitled to sit on the committee whose remit is the consideration of bills relating to Scotland as they pass through Parliament. With the advent of the Scottish Parliament, its purpose is limited although it is not defunct.

indeed other Scottish cities. A consultative council of leaders of civic and community and industrial life should be created and the Prime Minister should attend it at least once a year. These were just two of a number of suggestions and I remember referring to the first when I was travelling north with Donald Dewar in 1996. 'What would have happened if we had done something like that?' I asked. 'Well,' he replied, '"Yes" would have shot our fox.' And, of course, by then John Major had initiated Grand Committee meetings North of the Border and even sent the Stone of Scone.

But perhaps Margaret Thatcher's biggest single error was to impose the Poll Tax, as an experimental measure, in Scotland. As one of only two Tories who refused to support its imposition in Scotland, and who made opposition to English Poll Tax a main plank of my election address in 1987, I am not speaking with the benefit of hindsight.

It is nothing short of a political tragedy that a leader who achieved so much should have been so unable to grasp the importance of the Scottish dimension in United Kingdom politics. Just twenty years before she became leader the Conservative Party held a majority of seats in Scotland.

11

'Westminster' – a Pejorative Term

IN POLITICAL LIFE, it is only too easy to lose awareness of an issue and suddenly wake up to the fact that things have moved on. It was not until the early spring of 1989 that I had a rude awakening as to how far down the route I did not wish to travel things in Scottish affairs had progressed. I received a peremptory request from the Scottish Labour Party (i.e. Dewar, Gordon Brown et al.) that I should go and sign a document called *A Claim of Right for Scotland* on The Mound in Edinburgh and then attend a photo opportunity of all Scottish Labour MPs on 30 March 1989 at Arbroath – the venue for this photo opportunity was chosen because it was where the Declaration of Arbroath was signed by the (dubious) Scottish nobles of 1320. I was dismayed by what I was being requested to sign by the Labour Party that day. Since it was a hugely significant moment, I must dwell on it in detail.

As if by stealth, an organisation was born in 1980, styling itself the Campaign for a Scottish Assembly. Wrongly, as it transpired, I believed it was little more than a group of disgruntled people brandishing placards beside the old

Royal High School in Edinburgh, the venue of the assembly we never had. Alas, for my point of view, the Scottish Constitutional Convention arose out of the publication in July 1988 of *A Claim of Right for Scotland* by the Campaign for a Scottish Assembly. It recommended the creation of a convention by 'spontaneous action' whose purpose would be to bring about the creation of a Scottish assembly.

On the 30 March 1989 – symbolically the tenth anniversary of the defeat of the Labour government's devolution proposals when the 1979 referendum failed to produce the required majority in favour of the Scotland Act 1978 – the convention met for the first time. Canon Kenyon Wright – it was shrewd to have chosen a personally agreeable man of the cloth – chair of the Interim Working Committee, moved that the Convention adopt a declaration in the following terms:

> We, gathered as the Scottish Constitutional Convention, do hereby acknowledge the sovereign right of the Scottish people to determine the form of Government best suited to their needs, and do hereby declare and pledge that in all our actions and deliberations, their interests shall be paramount.
>
> We further declare and pledge that our actions and deliberations shall be directed to the following ends:
>
> - to agree a scheme for an Assembly or Parliament for Scotland;
> - to mobilise Scottish opinion and to ensure the approval of the Scottish people for that scheme;
> - to assert the right of the Scottish people to secure the implementation of that scheme.

The motion to adopt the declaration was supported by a range of speakers drawn from the political parties and other interests represented within the Convention, such as the Churches and the trades unions. At the conclusion of the debate, the Convention agreed unanimously to adopt the declaration in the terms outlined above. A representative of each organisation represented in the Convention then signed the declaration – and, of course, there was an abundance of photo opportunities. One, much used in the press over the following days, was of a seemingly happy band of Labour MPs. Dewar or his press officer claimed that there had been unanimous support from Scottish Labour MPs but eagle-eyed journalists spotted that there was an absentee – they could not make out the Member for Linlithgow among the cheerful Labour throng. (Inwardly, some Scottish Labour MPs were anything but cheerful but felt that they could not risk the wrath of some in their CLPs. Never underestimate the 'anything for a quiet life' factor in their constituency among Members of Parliament.)

My phone at home went red hot. First to call was the Press Association, asking where I had been to which I replied that I'd been doing my weekly constituency surgery at the community centre in Blackburn. I was asked if this was more important than the Convention and, to this, I gave a laconic 'Yes'. Next the journalist wanted to know if I agreed with what was decided. I asked for it to be read out to me. 'Gobbledegook,' I retorted, 'and I don't endorse gobble-degook – especially if it is one more mile down the motorway without exit to something indistinguishable from a separate Scottish state.' The press, not entirely hostile, had a field day – the statement that Labour MPs were unanimous was not quite right.

In retrospect, though not at the time, I regret my belligerence. It is never clever to provoke one's colleagues gratuitously. Dewar never forgave me. Our relations, already testy, had crossed the Rubicon. But, an infinitely more important Rubicon had been crossed. My considered opinion at the time and, of course, ever since was that sooner or later, after the event at The Mound on 30 March 1989, we would arrive at the situation of 18 September 2014. My only surprise is that the journey took as long as a quarter of a century.

In October 1989, the Scottish Constitutional Convention published *Towards a Scottish parliament: consultation document and report to the Scottish people*, which set out some of the thinking of the specialist working groups on the powers and functions of the Scottish parliament, financial issues, constitutional issues, women's issues and publicity and public involvement. The concept of a 'report to the Scottish people' reminded me of my visit with the Scottish Council for Development and Industry to Mao's China in 1971. It smacked of jargon and posturing – but doubtless it appealed to elements who had no responsibility for the realities of public life.

In November 1990, 'Key Proposals for Scotland's Parliament' was published by the Scottish Constitutional Convention. This recommended a directly elected Scottish Parliament, with the UK Parliament covering matters such as defence, foreign affairs, central economic and fiscal responsibilities and social security policy. It proposed that there should be the assignation of all Scottish income tax to Scotland's Parliament and, if possible, the assignation of all Scottish VAT as well.

Among the whole cascade of powers recommended for their Scottish Parliament, one in particular portended trouble: 'Powers to establish Scotland as a competitive and attractive location for companies to establish and to encourage competitive advantage for Scottish-based business.' I pointed out that Scotland could not expect a privileged position within the United Kingdom while, at the same time, enjoying the benefits of the Barnett formula. Dewar shrugged his shoulders – which is what he always did when confronted with an awkward question which he could not answer – and deftly changed the subject. One ought not to think ill of the dead but it really was wicked of Dewar to brush aside questions which he was too intelligent not to know required a substantial response.

I was publicly and privately scornful. Did those who endorsed these 'key proposals' have any idea of the gargantuan cost of disentangling the UK tax and fiscal regime? No, they did not. Had they consulted the Inland Revenue? No, they had not. I told Dewar that he should be ashamed of himself for allowing someone in his position as a member of the Shadow Cabinet to be seen as a 'fellow traveller' with all this nonsense. Our relations, already bad, became glacial. John Smith, as Shadow Chancellor, on the other hand, said with a disarming smile that he would rather not talk to me about the matter!

The Convention sought a directly elected Scottish Parliament within the United Kingdom – 'which, subject to the wishes of the people of Wales and the English regions would be the forerunner of Assemblies in these areas'. This revealed muddled and confused thinking. There was no question of the English regions following even the existing Scottish arrangement. 'If I were to go to Birmingham,' I said to colleagues, 'and told them that they should re-establish the Kingdom of Mercia, with different laws, a different education system and differences of many varieties from London and the rest of England, they would look at me in astonishment.'

Of course, almost everybody in England would like government brought closer to the people. But, as I have said countless times, this should be achieved by restoring dignity to the local authorities – the traditional English counties or metropolitan districts – not by creating a new layer of legislating politicians.

The Convention, preposterously, in my opinion, endorsed the principle of entrenchment, in relation to Scotland's parliament 'as regards its powers, the Scottish Executive, and Scotland's relationship with the United Kingdom Government, and the European Community in order that these would be incapable of being unilaterally amended at a later date by the Westminster Parliament'.

This was the first occasion that I clicked on to the fact that 'Westminster' had become a pejorative term, to be used frequently with a derogatory sneer. Those who formulated these proposals would clearly have had in mind something my father-in-law, the Lord Justice Clerk, John Wheatley, set forward in the Royal Commission on Local Government in Scotland, published in 1974. They would have discovered, as the Wheatley Commission did, that single-tier local government was unworkable and entirely inappropriate to the needs of the four levels of community as identified by Wheatley – the region, the district or shire, the locality and the parish.

One of the key issues of the recommendations which jarred with me, as the elected representative of the people of West Lothian in the United Kingdom Parliament, was that Canon Wright and his gang, under the heading 'Making the Scottish Parliament Truly Representative', had the effrontery to state:

1. The present 'first-past-the-post' electoral system is not acceptable for Scotland's Parliament and does not produce a truly representative assembly.

2. The Convention seeks for Scotland's Parliament an electoral system which should be assessed in terms of the following principles:–

   a. that it produces results in which the number of seats for the various parties is broadly related to the number of votes cast for them;

   b. that it ensures, or at least takes effective positive action to bring about equal representation of men and women, and encourage fair representation of ethnic and other minority groups;

   c. that it preserves a real link between the member and his/her constituency;

   d. that it is as simple as possible to understand;

   e. that it ensures adequate representation of less populous areas; and

   f. that the system be designed to place the greatest possible power in the hands of the electorate.[1]

Did an ex-missionary to India, who had metamorphosed into a Canon of Coventry Cathedral, think that my Scottish MP colleagues and I had failed to 'preserve a real link'? From his public statements, Wright gave me the impression that he did not know that most of the Westminster MPs he scorned return home on a Thursday night or Friday, hold surgeries for anyone to come to see them and dutifully attend local occasions, with at least monthly meetings of constituency parties or associations, often on a Sunday.

---

1   *Scottish Government Yearbook 1992*, pp 96–7.

I was present when the government's response to the Convention's consultation paper was given in December 1990. I tried to take part but Bernard Weatherill, the Speaker of the House, kindly told me in the corridor that he was sorry he couldn't call me because he had been so generous in calling me on two issues I had become deeply involved with – Iraq and Lockerbie – so other Scottish colleagues took precedence. I understood.

I quote at some length from the parliamentary debate to give a flavour of the obstinacy, justified in my view, of the Conservative government and to highlight arguments not just from my own perspective.

Mr Robert Maclennan (Liberal Democrat, Caithness, Sutherland and Easter Ross): To ask the Secretary of State for Scotland if he will make a statement on his response to the proposals of the Scottish Constitutional Convention?

Mr Ian Lang (Conservative, Secretary of State for Scotland): My views are well known. The organisation that calls itself the Scottish Constitutional Convention and its proposals are a distraction from the real issues which face the Scottish people.

Mr Maclennan: If the Secretary of State believes that proposals of the Scottish Constitutional Convention are not perfect, will he at least enter into dialogue with the political parties in Scotland which represent the overwhelming majority of the Scottish people? The Scottish people are persuaded that constitutional change to provide a democratic means of controlling the centralised administration is necessary to achieve the result to which the Government no doubt aspire. Why must we in Scotland, alone in western Europe, remain without proper democratic control over our Government when Spain, formerly the most centralised country in Europe, and

France, the next most centralised country, are both moving towards effective provincial government?

Mr Lang: If the hon. Gentleman regards those views as important, he has the opportunity to put them forward in a number of places – not least on the Floor of this House, in the mother of parliaments.

Mr Norman Hogg (Labour, Cumbernauld and Kilsyth): Is the Secretary of State aware that the organisation which calls itself the Scottish Constitutional Convention is representative of the Labour party, which sends 48 Members to the House, of the Liberal Democrats, who have a substantial and meaningful representation in the House, of the major Christian denominations in Scotland, of the trade unions and of the regional and district councils in Scotland? Whom does the Secretary of State think that he represents?

Mr Lang: I have the privilege to be the Secretary of State for Scotland and I thus represent Scotland and its people in the United Kingdom Parliament and in the United Kingdom Cabinet. What would happen to the Secretary of State for Scotland and his position in the Cabinet under the proposals of the Scottish Constitutional Convention? That is one of the fundamental questions that the body did not address.

Mr Alex Salmond (SNP, Banff and Buchan): Now that there are three identifiable positions on the constitutional question in Scottish politics – devolution advocated by the convention parties, no change advocated by the Secretary of State for Scotland and independence in Europe advocated by the Scottish National Party – why will not the Secretary of State for Scotland arrange to put the matter to the test and let the Scottish people decide on the three options in a fair referendum?

Mr Lang: It is well known that, because the present constitutional arrangements do not work to the SNP's advantage, it seeks to change them. SNP Members may call it independence in Europe; what they actually mean is the separation of Scotland from the rest of the United Kingdom, which would be immensely damaging for the people of Scotland.

Mr Andy Stewart (Conservative, Sherwood, Nottinghamshire, educated at Strathaven Academy in Lanarkshire and a Nottinghamshire farmer): Does my right hon. Friend agree that Scotland does not need another tier of Government – and certainly not one with the bureaucratic and interventionist aims put forward by the Convention?

Mr Lang: My hon. Friend is absolutely right. Not only would the Scottish Constitutional Convention add an extra tier of government, it would be an extra source of tax-raising designed to imposed [*sic*] an additional burden on the people of Scotland and to make it the highest-taxed part of the United Kingdom.[2]

The Scottish Constitutional Convention was also the subject of a Scottish Grand Committee debate in February 1992, in which Secretary of State for Scotland Ian Lang attacked the Convention's proposals principally on grounds of the financial impact on businesses and, in particular, that the resources asked for by those proposing a Scottish assembly would be in addition to the existing arrangements whereby the UK was spending £4 per head in England and £5 per head in Scotland.

I hope that the right hon. and learned Gentleman [John Smith] will take the opportunity to clarify the overall effect of

2   *Hansard*, 19 December 1990.

his United Kingdom tax proposals. Will he explain the eight new tax pledges that will add new tax burdens on the whole of the United Kingdom for the purpose of going some way to fund the £35 billion and more of increased spending that his hon. and right hon. Friends have promised? Will he make it clear how much freedom he, as Chancellor of the Exchequer, would grant in a Scottish Parliament or how much he would feel constrained by the separate entrenched powers that Opposition Members wish to set up?

We know answers to some of the questions. We know that the Opposition might allow tax to rise by as much as 3p in the pound. That would create a new position because, alone in the United Kingdom, Scots who pay income tax would pay more tax than their counterparts elsewhere in the United Kingdom. [*Interruption*] Opposition Members seem to find that amusing too. That policy would mean an extra £7 a week for a single man on average earnings which would be a separate burden that was not shared by others. Such a policy would raise only about £430 million, which is a fraction of the present Scottish Office budget.

I wonder whether the right hon. and learned Gentleman can guarantee that, given that position, those resources would be additional to the existing advantage that Scotland derives from the United Kingdom, whereby the United Kingdom Treasury continues to spend, for every £4 per head that it spends in England, £5 per head in Scotland. The benefit on identifiable public expenditure is £600 higher in Scotland than it is in England, 24 per cent higher and £500 higher than the average in the United Kingdom.

12

'Devolving Power-Making, Not the Right to Have an Opinion'

❖

MY ONLY CRUMB of comfort, in what seemed to be an ever lonelier position as an anti-devolutionist, was the strong suspicion that, should Neil Kinnock become prime minister, as I hoped, in 1992, he would, somehow or other, have kicked the issue into touch. And I stick to this opinion now. Years later, when I ran into him alone in New Palace Yard, after he had ceased to be party leader, I asked him: 'Neil, had you become prime minister, would you have implemented your public statements as Leader of the Opposition, acquiescing in devolution?' Kinnock replied that the whole devolution thing was the bollocks he and I knew it to be back in 1977–1978. This is not to say that he would not have been pressurised to the extent that a Kinnock government could not avoid bringing in legislation on Scotland but I like to think that Kinnock and his deputy leader, Roy Hattersley, would have found better legislation to promote in fields other than devolution.

But Kinnock resigned as leader of the party after losing the 1992 election and it was at this point that John Smith became leader. Sadly, his tenure was to prove brutally short and he died just two years later, on 12 May 1994. In that short time, he addressed many problems of party and country but one topic to which he did not give his mind to was devolution.

After John's moving funeral service at Cluny Parish Church in Edinburgh, my wife Kathleen and I were slowly walking up the hill accompanied by Sir Fitzroy Maclean, ex-MP for Bute and North Ayrshire, when we were overtaken by a colleague who, appearing somewhat shocked, said that he had heard Tony Blair was plotting to become leader 'before John was cold'. In the wheeling and dealing that was inevitably done before and subsequent to Blair's election to the leadership, it was decided that George Robertson, who had succeeded Tom Clarke, expert on the problems of the disabled, as Shadow Secretary of State for Scotland, should be confirmed in that post.

When Blair was elected as Smith's successor, I was in no position to go to talk to him in depth since he knew that I was one of a small minority of MPs who did not vote for him in the leadership contest. But my deduction is that he himself felt uncomfortable about a Scottish assembly/parliament but that it was not worth his having a humdinger of a row about it with Gordon Brown and Donald Dewar. Never underestimate the reluctance of politicians to square up to a fight with their colleagues.

When George Robertson became Shadow Secretary of State for Scotland, in the nicest possible way I am sure he would have liked me to retire – a troublesome voice would then be heard no more. But I had no intention of retiring, so the only way I could be silenced would be for me to be deselected in advance of endorsement as a parliamentary candidate for the forthcoming 1997 general election. This meant undermining me in the West Lothian Constituency Labour Party. But this would have been extraordinarily difficult since I had been an extremely assiduous MP, not only in my constituency role but also in never failing to be present at and giving a Parliamentary report to the Sunday afternoon monthly meetings of West Lothian Constituency Labour Party, at the headquarters in Bridge Street, Bathgate. Their only possible chance of de-stooling me was deftly to organise a number of trade union and dormant trade union delegates to attend the selection conference, under instructions to vote in favour of another selection conference at which I would be only one of the candidates – and greatly humiliated. This plotting was easily stymied. I was also led to believe that, since George Robertson in a previous incarnation had been the Scottish organiser for the trade union GMB, my friend the GMB general secretary, David Basnett, had a word in his ear to the effect that it would not be clever to try to get Tam Dalyell de-selected for the 1997 election.

It is well known that a significant number of Scottish Labour MPs in the 1990s were acutely uncomfortable about the direction the Labour Party in Scotland was taking on the formation of a Scottish parliament. Why was it then that their ill-concealed private misgivings were not translated into public opposition? Part of the answer is that they felt that their political backs were not protected in their own constituencies. I was lucky in the mature political calibre of the officers of the West Lothian Constituency Labour Party and wise in gaining the friendship and understanding of the trade union leaders.

I am not completely certain what George Robertson really felt about devolution in the years from 1993 to 1997 when he was Shadow Secretary of State for Scotland – nor, I suspect, was he. Outwardly, he had to display enthusiasm for a Scottish assembly. And, remember, that his constituency was Hamilton – the very town where Winnie Ewing had won her remarkable by-election victory. Robertson was elected in May 1978, in a bitterly contested by-election. What I am sure about, fast-forward 20 years, is that, in the summer of 2014, no one was more vehement in denouncing the Yes Campaign than Lord Robertson of Port Ellen, Knight of the Thistle, former Defence Secretary, 1997–99, and former Secretary General of NATO, 1999–2003. The impression I had, in the years from 1995 to 1997 – and I do not think my impression is an unfair one since it was shared by some of my other Parliamentary Labour Party colleagues – was that George Robertson was not a true believer in a Scottish assembly or its merits but saw that the creation of an assembly would, in his famous words, 'kill nationalism stone dead'. But then, within the Labour movement at that period, the idea that an assembly set up by the Labour Party would dish the nationalists once and for all was one that was commonly held. It was a strategic political device, not political belief.

I surmise that, on the formation of a Labour government, Donald Dewar and Gordon Brown came to the conclusion that Robertson, as the Shadow Secretary of State for Scotland, was not the vehicle to drive through their proposed Scotland Bill. So they persuaded Tony Blair that, in the event of a Labour win at the next general election, Robertson should go to his first love – defence and relations with the United States – and that Dewar, by this time Opposition Chief Whip, should himself be responsible for the contentious Scottish legislation.

I learned that, even so, Blair took some persuading over this. After all, he was a County Durham MP and the idea of yielding supposed advantages to the Scots would not have been exactly appealing when his seat was so close to the border. Other MPs representing constituencies in the north-east had certainly felt this way before. It was a matter of irony that John Smith's most determined critic amongst north of England Labour MPs was Harry Cowans who had inherited Ted Short's Central Newcastle seat. Cowans, a Geordie through and through, spoke his mind. He told Smith and the rest of us in December 1976 that Short's and now his Constituency Labour Party were totally against Scottish devolution. What they wanted, he said, was more powers, particularly more money for the Newcastle City Council.

Although he had not been in Parliament between 1977 and 1979 during the run-up to the 1979 referendum, Blair was sceptical about devolution – I gathered this from what he told me personally and it was confirmed by Derek Foster, Chief Whip and MP for Bishop Auckland. However, he acquiesced in the Dewar–Brown proposal. I blame Blair for many things he was to do as prime minister – I do not blame him for this. Devolution was party policy. Senior Cabinet colleagues were jumping up and down. What else was the prime minister to do other than allow them to forge ahead?

Even though devolution was listed in the newspapers as number 19 on the list of election priorities, from the moment that Friday morning in May when the 1997 election results were announced with a Labour majority of 179, I knew that the game was up and that opposition to devolution was just impossible. I am a Pym-ite in these matters. Francis Pym, Mrs Thatcher's second foreign secretary, opined (much to her consternation) that, in British politics, majorities over 50 are unhealthy. With a slender majority, frustrating a guillotine motion on the discussion of a proposed bill might just have been possible. With a majority of 179, many of whom were newcomers to Parliament, a successful challenge to the government's will was impossible.

Shortly after Labour's victory, a bill was concocted promising a Scottish government. The parliamentarians working on the bill allowed their unease about their work to be known. And, given the experience of 1977, a guillotine motion was rapidly introduced. Unlike 1978, it was absolutely impossible to muster sufficient MPs to defeat a guillotine motion, which would have meant that discussion on a constitutional bill would go on and on and on, on the floor of the House of Commons. It was at this point that Labour Party sowed the seeds of its own destruction. Dewar and Henry McLeish, Minister of State for Scotland with responsibility for home affairs and devolution, knew that, if they did not get their devolution proposals through quickly, in an another three months, they would not get them through at all because new English MPs would have found their feet and raised awkward questions. I bore little grudge. In 1978, Labour MPs were battle-hardened veterans of many a political controversy, scrap or political fisticuffs. In 1998, new MPs, ambitious for preferment, can be excused for not wishing to get across the Party leadership and whips, with possible terminal effect on their careers. And for what? In 1978 the size of the slim majority meant that diversity votes could be effective. In 1998, given the landslide majority, there was no chance of defiance succeeding and I understood perfectly well why they so desperately wanted me to 'retire'. They just thought – with good reason – that I would and could do 1979, all over again.

The Scotland Bill was the child of a Cabinet committee set

up under the chairmanship of the Lord Chancellor, Derry Irvine. In the course of an interview with Professor Lord Peter Hennessy on Monday 13 December 2014, on Radio 4, Robin Butler (Lord Butler of Brockwell) volunteered that the Cabinet committee had been a great success. An old friend, I asked him whether it was true that, as Jack Straw had let it be known, Lord Irvine had been reluctant to ask the awkward questions that, as Lord Chancellor, he should have asked, on account of his delicate personal relations with Donald Dewar, the Secretary of State for Scotland and sponsor of the legislation. Irvine's chairmanship skills are not in doubt. I asked Lord Butler if he was carrying out the Lord Chancellor's duty as devil's advocate. Butler then referred me to my old friend of Scottish Office days, Kenneth MacKenzie, who had been the secretary of the Cabinet committee. When I phoned Irene MacKenzie, she told me that, alas, her husband was very ill but she would ask him. She phoned me back and said that her husband – in my experience among the straightest and most honourable of civil servants – understandably preferred not to discuss professional matters in his retirement. For clarity, we must await the eventual publication of the minutes – and even then we might not be much the wiser.

During the passage of the 1997 Scotland Bill, I pleaded, on the occasions I was called, with pro-assembly colleagues to 'be careful what you wish for on more powers'. It fell on deaf ears. I just wanted those who were foisting this dog's breakfast of devolution on the country to stop and think of the consequences of their actions. And, as one of those doing the foisting, Gordon Brown might care to reflect that, years later, his 'vows', promised days before the 2014 independence referendum, were not approved by the Parliament of the

United Kingdom. Much of the current constitutional wrangling is a consequence of the Labour government's haste in establishing devolved Parliaments. The stakes are too high to make the same mistake again. Politicians should calm down and slow down.

The bill was a parliamentary travesty and another disgrace to the House of Commons. Predictable and predicted, foreseeable and foreseen, many important clauses went undiscussed. At no stage was it fully appreciated that more powers for the Scottish Parliament would have wider repercussions and were bound to blow open the West Lothian question. Inevitably this would lead to the diminution of Scots MPs at Westminster.

Timed to the limit, the guillotine fell. Moreover, the allocation of time was meagre as the Labour government, rightly and understandably, had legislation in other subjects competing for parliamentary time. My own role was that of an ever-present spectator. When Dewar could not be on the frontbench, Henry McLeish, who guided the bill through, ruthlessly arranged for garrulous pro-devolution MPs to spin out the time, talking constitutional gibberish, while any of us who were likely to raise seriously awkward questions were frozen out by the clock. In vain did I remind Dewar – a well-read man – of Richard Burdon Haldane in 1918 and his 'Report of the Machinery of Government Committee': 'We have come to the conclusion that in the sphere of Civil Government, the duty of investigation and thought as preliminary to action, might with great advantage be more definitely recognised.'

Madam Speaker Boothroyd, a close friend since our days together on the National Executive Committee of the Labour Party in the 1980s, took me aside, saying, 'I see exactly the game that they are playing but I and my deputy speakers are bound to share out such back-bench time as there is between all Scottish MPs – whether they have thought about the subject or not.' I could not argue that she was wrong.

The vote on the Scotland Bill was little more than a formality. The huge Labour majority filed through the parliamentary lobby in support. Little did they know what they were doing. And, unlike in 1979, when the question was put to the people on 11 September 1997, the results were overwhelmingly in support of a devolved parliament, with 75 per cent of those who voted in favour and a 'Yes' vote in every part of the country. The second question in the referendum, as to whether the parliament should have tax-levying powers, was also answered affirmatively except in Dumfries and Galloway and in Orkney.

While I watched him glumly on the television during the opening of the Scottish Parliament on 1 July 1999, Dewar clearly enjoyed announcing, 'There shall be a Scottish Parliament.' and the rejoicing by the crowds milling around in the High Street of Edinburgh was ecstatic. The scene was akin to those in a city centre after the local football team has won the cup. The basis of Dewar's triumphalism of course lay in the huge victory in the 1997 referendum. I was not in the least surprised at the referendum results, as parliamentary debate had been stifled. Dewar was able to portray those of us against devolution to an Edinburgh Parliament as being anti-Scottish. Anti-Scottish we were not. We saw opposing the establishment of a parliament in Edinburgh as being in the real best interests of people in Scotland.

❖

This is not the place to go into a discussion of the workings, achievements or shortcomings of the Holyrood Parliament or of the massive costs involved as the building of it went hugely over-budget.[1] I am not qualified to do so as I have darkened its portals only twice – once for a reception given by the Scottish Council for Development and Industry of which I was president for three years and, as such, I had to perform the duties of host, and once for a tête-à-tête dinner with the Rt Hon. George Reid, my friend and political opponent, when he was Presiding Officer of the Parliament. But I take the opportunity to say that, from the outside, it looks to me that MSPs are generally hard-working men and women of neither higher nor lower calibre than Westminster MPs.

But I shudder at the cost to public funds of running the Parliament, its maintenance and the cost of a panoply of politicians, their researchers and their secretaries, amounting to many times those of the Scotland Office at Dover House with its Secretary of State, a Minister of State in the Commons, another in the Lords and a brace of Under-Secretaries of State, who served Scotland well in the 20th century and who have both fought and delivered for Scotland.

Be that as it may, I want to make two points which are

---

1   When I raised the issue of the building costs, Donald Dewar went on the *Today* programme to tell listeners that I was 'wicked and alarmist' in suggesting that the cost of the Holyrood building might be over £40 million (original estimates were between £10 million and £40 million). Knowing from Jim Stretton (Chief Executive, UK Operations, of Standard Life and Member of the Court of the Bank of England) that their Lothian Road building had cost Standard Life £100 million plus, I suggested the parliament might cost £200 million. Even I did not think it would exceed the upper estimate by almost eleven-fold, ending up at just over at £414 million! And this was just the building itself.

important to the underlying theme of the book. The Scottish Parliament was set up on the assumption that Labour would eternally be in power in Scotland or, at the very least, be the leading party in a coalition. Labour have, in fact, been the government in power for just half of the parliament's existence. That the SNP have formed the government in Scotland since 2007 has destroyed the myth of Labour dominance and given rise to exactly the constitutional crisis that I have been warning of for decades. And of course, as predicted, the inevitable problems caused by the very existence of a Scottish Parliament and a Welsh Assembly were quickly felt at Westminster. No one was aware of this more pertinently than the Speaker, Betty Boothroyd, who succinctly expressed the dilemma in her book *Betty Boothroyd: The Autobiography*:

> After the first elections to the new Scottish Parliament and the Welsh Assembly the Commons ran into problems with its own constitutional settlement. Anomalies were bound to arise from transferring responsibility for substantial issues like health, education, social services, transport and domestic law from Westminster to Edinburgh. The Welsh Assembly in Cardiff had lesser powers of policy-making but, even there, many local matters that Welsh MPs had put to Welsh ministers at Westminster were no longer our concern.
>
> Tam Dalyell's famous West Lothian question remained unanswered: why should Scots and Welsh MPs have the right to intervene in purely English affairs, whereas English MPs have no right to intervene in similar issues decided in Edinburgh and Cardiff? Short of setting up a devolved English Parliament, which was not being proposed, there is no real answer to that.
>
> Devolution complicated my task, making it harder to select MPs in debates to ensure the right balance between the regions

and increasing the pressure on my discretionary powers. Friction was inevitable.

After complaints about the scope of Welsh questions, I issued new guidelines on 12 July 1999 stipulating that Commons questions must relate to matters for which ministers were responsible. That meant limiting the range of questions to Scottish and Welsh ministers at Westminster and refusing questions that related to devolved policy and detailed expenditure.

Tam Dalyell asked if the Scottish Parliament would observe the same self-denying ordinance in respect of UK matters beyond its competence. All I could say was that the new Commons guidelines would be sent to Edinburgh, but I was happy to leave that conundrum to Sir David Steel, presiding officer of the new Scottish Parliament. That displeased some Scots MPs, who accused me of silencing their right to speak on Scottish matters. 'We were devolving power-making, not the right to have an opinion,' said one. The right to hold opinions, however, was not at stake. My guidelines concerned questions to Ministers about their specific responsibilities. We could not carry on after devolution as if nothing had happened.

13

'Just Say Naw'

❖

I RETIRED FROM the House of Commons at the 2005 general election. A number of key members of the Linlithgow Constituency Labour Party, including Neil Findlay, now a prominent MSP, told me they would be happy if I should contest the boundary-changed seat of Linlithgow and Falkirk East. I thanked them and declined. Much better that constituents should ask themselves, 'Why does Tam Dalyell have to go?' rather than, at the end of the next parliament, 'Why did the old fart, at seventy-seven, have to hang on?'

Within a few months, it came home to me how different the perspective of politics from outside the Commons was and I soon lost touch with the ins-and-outs of day-to-day political life. While I was an MP, many former friends and colleagues visiting the parliamentary precinct had told me that this was precisely their experience. Moreover, in recent years, the Scottish press, doubtless constrained by the dire financial circumstances of the newspaper industry, has virtually ignored Scottish-related business in the House of Commons in favour of the decisions and machinations of the Holyrood Parliament. As a result, my direct involvement with the evolution of devolution, post 2005, has been considerably less but, of course, I have been watching closely from the sidelines and there are two key events which have occurred since 2005 about which I must comment.

The first was the Commission on Scottish Devolution set up in 2008 under the chairmanship of Sir Kenneth Calman, distinguished oncologist, vice-chancellor of the University of Durham and later Chancellor of the University of Glasgow. The purpose was clear: 'to review the provisions of the Scotland Act 1998 in the light of experience and to recommend any changes to the present constitutional arrangements that would enable the Scottish Parliament to serve the people of Scotland better, improve the financial accountability of the Scottish Parliament and continue to secure the position of Scotland within the United Kingdom.' The terms of reference were consensus – all views were to be represented and evidence was to be called for. The first evidence to be sent was from me and Calman said that I would be invited to give oral evidence, yet no invitation came. (To his great credit, Calman himself took the train to Linlithgow to have a two-hour discussion with me.) Later, it transpired that, at an early meeting of the Commission, the members agreed, 'We don't want Dalyell.'

My opinion that the existence of the Scottish Parliament should be called into question was inconvenient and should not be heard. In November 2015, I asked Calman for his reflections on the achievement of the commission. 'It brought politicians of different persuasions together. It should be that devolution was possible.' was the answer. When I suggested to him that the crucial ingredient of good will was absent, he gave an assenting sigh.

However, there was one happening which left me perplexed.

No, more than perplexed – astounded. This was the so-called Edinburgh Agreement between the United Kingdom government and the Scottish government on a referendum on independence for Scotland, signed with much fanfare in Edinburgh on 15 October 2012, by David Cameron, Prime Minister, Michael Moore, then Secretary of State for Scotland, Alex Salmond, First Minister of Scotland, and his deputy, Nicola Sturgeon.

The preamble blandly asserts that '[t]he United Kingdom Government and the Scottish Government have agreed to work together to ensure that a referendum on Scottish independence can take place'. 'What consultation had taken place on such a referendum, with the Members of the House of Commons or House of Lords?' I wondered. Cursory enquiring of friends in Parliament, a rapidly decreasing band, revealed that they thought that there had been no consultation whatsoever with backbenchers. As one friend put it, 'As far as I'm concerned, the notion of a referendum has been cooked up between No. 10 Downing Street and the First Minister's residence in Charlotte Square.' But, he added, 'It's OK because, in a referendum, those in favour of separation will get slaughtered three to one!' I told him that I was not quite so sure because referenda are seldom wholly what they purport to be about.[1]

---

1 Fast-forward to September 2014 and it was clear to me that such majorities as the Yes campaign had in Dundee, Glasgow, North Lanarkshire and West Dunbartonshire were less about the future constitutional arrangements of the United Kingdom and the fiscal powers to be accorded to the Scottish Parliament than about the poor housing conditions, underfunded schools and unsatisfactory health and transport conditions in those areas. It seems clear to me that these are precisely the kinds of issues the SNP government

.It then transpired that Cameron had agreed that the referendum 'be legislated for by the Scottish Parliament'. Did Downing Street not click on to the nature of the present that they were handing to the SNP government – that they would be able to frame the question in the referendum to their own maximum advantage? I thought that my first prime minister, the worldly-wise Harold Macmillan, must have been turning in his grave at the naivety of his Conservative successor.

The Edinburgh Agreement stated that the referendum should 'be conducted so as to command the confidence of parliaments, governments and people', further stating that it should 'deliver a fair test and a decisive expression of the views of people in Scotland and a result that everyone will respect'. In February 2012, I thought that this was an aspiration which was certain to be unfulfilled – and I said so to the press. To me, it was clear that a simple majority one way or the other was all that was required for this aspect of the agreement to fail – in other words, the machinery for the dismantling of the United Kingdom could be set in motion by a handful of votes.

It has always seemed strange to me that the Edinburgh Agreement did not include the constitutional requirement of a two-thirds majority for the result. Any major change should not take place on the basis of threadbare majorities. When I spoke to him recently, the distinguished professor of politics

---

could have addressed with their existing powers. But of course they would argue that only with full independence would they be able to deal with them. Whilst everyone would agree that poverty, unemployment and education standards need to be addressed, the SNP's targeting, during the referendum campaign, of the unemployed, materially poor and disenfranchised with the promise of a better life in an independent Scotland was extraordinarily cynical.

Philip Norton reeled off to me a long list of countries where a 66 per cent majority of the electorate was required for a change in the constitution to be enacted – Germany, Italy, Norway, Hungary and Finland, to name but a few. Sweden requires a 75 per cent majority, and only Brazil was lower, with 60 per cent. If the United Kingdom is to be torn asunder, it is not unreasonable to require a 66 per cent majority for such an action. Even many local organisations and associations like golf clubs and Rotary Clubs up and down the land require a two-thirds majority for any change to their constitution.

The SNP's vision for an independent Scotland was summed up in *Scotland's Future: Your Guide to an Independent Scotland*, published in November 2013. This was the key document in the Yes campaign's armoury. This so-called White Paper on independence was an expensive travesty. Funded by taxpayers and written by supposedly neutral civil servants, it was, in fact, an SNP tract. It was complete and utter fabrication concocted for purely political purposes. The SNP government has never hesitated to use public money for party political purposes nor have the backbench committees of the Holyrood Parliament exerted a beady eye, as it was hoped they would, on the activities of Holyrood. And, in 2015, in a political climate akin to a one-party state, it was even less likely that they would do so.

Albeit I am a friend of Alastair Darling and an admirer of his financial management of the economic crisis of 2008, I declined to have anything to do with the Better Together campaign during the run-up to the referendum. (My wife and I gave a modest amount of money to those who were organising

George Galloway's 'Just Say Naw' tours of Scotland.) From the very formation of Better Together, I was dismayed by their undertakings to delegate further powers to the Scottish Parliament, which I knew could not be implemented without reverberations throughout the United Kingdom. Frankly, considering the views I held, I thought that it would be fraudulent and deceitful for me to sign up to their agenda.

I hear voices rebuking me, saying, 'But, Mr Dalyell, why did you fail to make your views known in August and September 2014?' For the imperatively good reason that there were thousands of excellent people canvassing on the doorsteps, trying to keep the United Kingdom together. It would have been clumsy, to the point of wickedness, if I had aired my view of Better Together's promises. So, for five days running, before the vote, I declined pressing invitations from Ian Katz, editor of *Newsnight*, to be interviewed by that most skilful at eliciting the true feelings of interviewees, the BBC's special correspondent, Allan Little. I had no such dilemma with BBC Scotland since they did not approach me once – unlike Radio Wales and several English regions of the BBC – during the run-up to the vote.

After high-profile television debates and polls showing a narrowing of opinion between the 'Yes' and 'No' camps as referendum day drew closer, panic took over. Counter-productively, Cameron, Clegg and Miliband, blew into Scotland at the eleventh hour and fifty-ninth minute, for the Union cause and blew out again. Their efforts, which might have been effective six weeks earlier, were simply too little too late and made them look like gauche laughing stocks. But then panic has been the source of so much trouble in the devolutionary story for over 50 years!

But much more serious was the last-minute intervention of

Gordon Brown with the 'Vow'. Self-appointed and wanting a role in which he would be seen to turn the tide in favour of a 'No' vote, Brown gave hostages to fortune, conceding hitherto uncovenanted powers for the Scottish Parliament which, I fear, will lead to recriminations about the politics of betrayal for years to come. The party leaders were, all three of them, crazy to give promises which threaten the fragility of the United Kingdom and doubly crazy to allow people to think that Brown was their spokesman. Within not months, not days but hours of the announcement of the referendum result (55 per cent 'No' and 45 per cent 'Yes') – an unequivocal victory for the 'No' voters which, in other contexts, such as a US presidential election, would have been described as a landslide – it became only too apparent that 'a result that everyone will respect' was as far from being achieved as ever.

Whilst I always knew that pro-independence supporters would find a 'No' vote impossible to stomach, what I – and, I suspect, anyone else – did not foresee was the levels of bitterness and grievance and the sense of betrayal that would ensue. It had already begun during the referendum campaign with very public comments on Twitter about bestselling author and creator of Harry Potter, J.K. Rowling. After it became known that she had donated £1 million to the Better Together campaign, she was accused of being a traitor whose books should be burned in public. Indeed, Scotland is now littered with cases of deep unpleasantness, the like of which have not surfaced before. Glasgow-born and -bred Michelle Mone, founder of the lingerie company Ultimo, was called a 'cow' and 'slut' and comments like 'We'll come and get you' were directed at her on Twitter and social media in response to her support for the Union. Can we be surprised that Michelle Mone has since moved her business to London because, to her dismay, Scotland under the SNP was becoming, to use her words, 'a place consumed by vitriolic hatred and ill-will'? Others have quietly followed suit and slipped south.

Even Nick Robinson's cancer of the throat was not sufficient to deter social media thugs opining that the BBC political editor's illness was karma for what they saw as his biased coverage of the referendum. Nor has the abuse abated since the 2015 general election. In June 2015, Alice Thomson wrote in *The Times*, 'One executive of a FTSE 100 company that supported a "no" vote in the referendum admitted they are still paying a high price. "We had no idea we would be on the receiving end of so much bile and vitriol. Our senior managers [currently based in Scotland] are queuing up to move."'

Perhaps most outrageous of all was the barbaric treatment meted out to the former Liberal Democrat leader, the late Charles Kennedy – as demonstrated in an article in *The Times* written by Alice Thomson:

> Charles Kennedy was stoical when he lost his Ross, Skye and Lochaber seat after 32 years. His father had recently died, his brother had been paralysed after a stroke and his career was in tatters but he praised his SNP opponent full-heartedly, joking that Scotland was undergoing a 'night of the sgian dubhs'.
>
> Yet a few hours later he came home to his grandfather's crofthouse to find his bins had been overturned and rubbish smeared around his drive. A campaign started on Twitter lambasting him for being a 'sore loser'.
>
> Kennedy was an alcoholic but he was always charming, never abusive.
>
> Once when we were both meant to be doing Radio 4's *Any Questions* he missed three trains because he said he couldn't find the entrance to Euston Station. He never arrived but he sent me a funny apology.
>
> Opposition to him during the last election, however, was

bitter and vile. One SNP supporter tweeted that he was 'a drunken alcoholic arsehole' while another called him an 'alkie c***'. Brian Smith, an SNP campaigner, tweeted more than 100 times during the campaign about the 'quisling' MP, saying he was not fit for Westminster.[2]

Perhaps I should add that I am told I have also attracted a cascade of unflattering abuse on social media. But, then, I am a disciple of Clement Attlee in these matters. When told by his press secretary, Francis Williams, that the *Daily Herald* and other papers had written terrible criticisms of the prime minister, Attlee responded, 'Is that so? Francis, pass me the Births, Marriages and Deaths – and the cricket scores.'

---

2 Alice Thomson, 'Sturgeon must stop the vicious SNP bullies', *The Times*, 10 June 2015.

14

Independence by the Back Door

❖

ALTHOUGH I HADN'T been directly involved in public debate before the referendum, my opinion was sought soon after the event. Donald Macintyre, veteran political journalist of *The Independent*, put a legitimate direct question to me: 'Mr Dalyell, if you were prime minister, what would you do?' When most politicians are confronted with a question, they either can't or don't want to answer, they intone, 'We are very clear . . .' Well, I am genuinely *very* clear. I would seize the bull by the horns and set in motion the re-establishment of the principles of regional devolution. I recognise that it would be extremely difficult to cobble together, in any precise way, the former regions set up by the Wheatley Commission in 1975. Time has moved on. But time has also moved on in England with the creation of northern powerhouses such as Manchester. This would mean a substantial amount of the powers now vested in Holyrood would be handed over to the appropriate local authorities in Scotland – Strathclyde (maybe with Ayrshire separated), Lothian, Central, Fife, Tayside, Dumfries and Galloway, Grampian, Highland, the Western Isles, Orkney and Shetland – and, in England, to metropolitan regions, such as Birmingham, Manchester and Sheffield, and, where appropriate, to the English counties, with which English people tend to identify. This would meet the real demand to bring government nearer to local people. The 'powers' which concern 99 per cent of the population are local – quasi-managerial in that they are not the powers of the Edinburgh Parliament.

What did happen, of course, was that the hastily convened Smith Commission, which began its cross-party talks little more than a month after the referendum in order to codify the airy promises of further devolutionary powers as espoused in the 'Vow', published its recommendations with such astonishing haste that it was bound to unravel.

The 'Smith Commission Report' is a curious, shallow document and it presented an economic nightmare. Smith adopted the idea that had been milling around in Conservative circles for years – that power over all income tax, apart from setting the threshold at which tax becomes payable, should be devolved to Scotland. The proposal looked ever so convenient in that it would appear to solve the Tories' problem in Scotland – that, in a parliament which only decides how to spend money, there is no room for a party whose main raison d'être is to promote a tax-cutting agenda. So give it sweeping powers over income tax and, all of a sudden, the Tories in Scotland will be seen to have a meaningful role. But, economically, it just does not add up and, in the not-so-long term, it would be politically suicidal for the Union. An example: let us suppose that a UK government raises income tax in order to pay for some UK purpose – perhaps extra defence spending or paying down the national debt. This tax increase would not apply to Scotland but people in Scotland would benefit without having to pay for it. Such a situation is certainly detrimental to the rest of UK taxpayers. To redress this, the solution would be to cut Scotland's Treasury block grant by an amount equivalent to that that the tax increase would raise in Scotland. The Scottish government would then have to decide to meet the spending shortfall by either raising income tax or cutting spending, certainly with regard to local authorities that are already at the end of their tether.

Fair enough, some might think, but what if the UK government's extra spending was to pay for the bombing of Syria or Trident? How acceptable would that be to Scottish opinion? The political ramifications are obvious – the Union would be in perilous danger. This is why, on 17 November 2015, the Lords Economic Affairs Committee sought to halt the Scotland Act 2015 legislative process. The Lords demanded that, until a clear practical framework for implementing the Smith financial proposals is established, there should be a pause. The Commons are passing into law a bill, based on Smith, with no clear idea on how it will actually work. The truth is that no other government in the entire world has such a tax scheme – for a very good reason. These proposals cause so many problems that they simply do not work. At best, the Smith Commission should be re-convened to come up with an alternative tax package that will work – if such a thing could possibly exist.

Despite such obvious flaws, perhaps the most extraordinary thing about the Smith Commission is that it is surely based on a false premise for, in Chapter 2, paragraph 20 refers to 'the sovereign right of the people of Scotland to determine the form of government best suited in their needs, as expressed in the referendum on 18th September 2014'. How can Smith make out that this was 'expressed' in a referendum where the question was 'Should Scotland be an independent country?' and the answer was a decisive 'No'.

We have no evidence to show how many of the 'No' voters wanted more devolved power to the Edinburgh Parliament. Many, in fact, probably wanted less power devolved to an Edinburgh Parliament and a SNP government which they opposed. Hundreds of thousands of Scots, ever since 1977, have been concerned about the knock-on effects on other parts of the United Kingdom and the creeping feeling that increased powers actually mean independence by the back door.

But credit to Lord Smith – he stuck to the timetable which was imposed upon him. However, the Smith Commission was yet another political party stitch-up, aided by so-called 'civic Scotland', a nebulous term which is actually just a construct for commentators to use for their own political ends. Ideally, Baron Smith of Kelvin should have taken the time to wander round Scotland observing the mood of the country and talking to local people as Lord Wheatley did during the two years of hatching the Royal Commission on Local Government Reform, rather than gleaning public opinion by sifting through emails and letters. Had he done so, he would have discovered that far from all the 55 per cent 'No' voters wanted massive new powers, especially when nobody has defined what 'devo max' actually entails. Had the question of more devolved powers been on the ballot paper in 2014, the 'Yes' campaigners might have got an even bigger shock.

15

The 'Once in a Generation' Question

❖

I AM AFRAID that historians may conclude that the seeds of David Cameron's remarkable and unanticipated (by most) election victory in May 2015 were planted at 7.00 a.m. on 19 September 2014. Spurning advice which beseeched him not to, Cameron pranced out on to the steps of Downing Street two hours after the result of the referendum, saying into the battery of microphones that the 'West Lothian question' had to be addressed and promising 'English votes for English laws'. Naked opportunism! His purpose can only have been to ensure that the Conservatives rather than UKIP could play the English card. It allowed the SNP to snatch an incredible general election victory in May 2015, from the jaws of defeat in the referendum of September 2014. Cameron had handed the SNP a new grievance. His reckless pledge about 'English votes for English laws' the morning after the referendum gave the SNP the boost it needed. Begged by Alastair Darling at 5 a.m. to be conciliatory, he declined to be so.

Although right up until the election itself, opinion polls were suggesting the possibility of a hung parliament, the actual result was a Conservative majority of 12. The Conservatives won 331 seats (up 24), Labour had 232 (down 26), the Liberals won 8 seats (down 49) and the SNP took 56 seats (up 50), taking all but 3 seats in Scotland. The results did not surprise me. All the opinion polls and the exit polls had got it badly wrong. Why had this happened?

Vince Cable, the Liberal Democrat veteran, blamed a Tory campaign 'based on people's fear of a Labour government and the Scottish nationalists'. At the time, I watched a BBC One news item investigating why the Conservatives had made a clean sweep of the Liberal Democrat seats in Cornwall, Devon and Somerset. Vox pop indicated that an overwhelming reason was concern over a Labour government, orchestrated by the Scottish National Party. For many voters in England, therefore, the only way to prevent the SNP from being powerbrokers was to vote Conservative.[1]

But the situation in Scotland is more complex. Why did Scots vote decisively against independence in the 2014 referendum and then sign up in droves for the party that proposes independence? On the face of it, this seems perverse. But, actually, it is explicable and there are a number of reasons for it.

Throughout the election campaign in spring 2015, Nicola Sturgeon was at pains to stress that the SNP campaign was not a rerun of the independence referendum campaign and should not be seen as such. The election was to be fought and won on the basis of standing up for Scotland. So, many thousands of Scots, who would never vote for independence

---

1   Despite the rise in the UKIP vote in the north of England, the Oldham by-election of December 2015 demonstrated that the appeal of UKIP to Labour voters was far less than anticipated.

and having voted 'No' in the referendum, thinking that was now all settled and behind them, lent their support to SNP candidates, who would go to Westminster 'to stand up' for Scotland. But, for others, when independence was rejected on 18 September 2014, a continuing movement was created, which has no interest in making this distinction. The general election of 2015 was the next staging post for these people – the self-styled '45' which refers to the percentage of people who had supported independence.

But there are other reasons. It is impossible to exaggerate the ineptness of the Labour television campaign. By some alchemy, Jim Murphy, my nice Scottish whip 2003–2005, whom I liked, was handed the poisoned chalice of leading Scottish Labour. He will be remembered for jogging, kicking a football and twirling a balloon in front of kids on television, rather than delivering a political message. Many Labour activists cringed and declined to campaign. Sturgeon herself was a plausible but under-interrogated performer. But she was able as party leader (though not a candidate) to exploit the podium. It might have been an altogether different matter if some of the sharp junior MPs, like Tom Greatrex, Gregg McClymont and Ian Murray, had been able to tackle her on the record of the SNP government at Holyrood over the preceding years.

But there were other factors. In former Labour First Minister Jack McConnell's opinion, the 'Vow', enunciated by Gordon Brown, entrenched the perception that Labour was working hand in hand with the Tories and provided a good reason for erstwhile Labour voters to vote SNP in a Westminster election for the first time in many years. This was not the first time this observation had been made.

There has always been a fundamental difficulty for Labour

opponents of devolution. Back in the 1970s, we were acutely sensitive to jibes from within the Labour Party that we were 'getting into bed with the Tories'. These came, in particular, from Jim Sillars and the party chairman, Bob Thompson, both of whom were to become champions of a 'Yes' vote in the 2014 referendum, and, ironically, from George Galloway, who, with Brian Wilson, in 2014, was, by far and away, the most effective 'Just Say No' campaigner. And, actually, it was on this issue that the ill-conceived 'Better Together Campaign' came unstuck. Gordon Brown's 'Vow' was supposed to bring prodigal Labour sons and daughters back into the 'Labour fold'. That it did nothing of the kind is neither here nor there. Forty years ago, George Cunningham and I had deep discussions on tactics. As our 'Tory partners', we chose those who were honourable, were committed to the preservation of the Union and, above all, knew how to keep their mouths shut at critical moments. They were some of the super grandees of the Conservative Party – Julian Amery, his colleague and friend, Fitzroy Maclean, Airey Neave, Maurice Macmillan (son of the ex-prime minister), Hugh Fraser and Neil Marten. George Cunningham and I were very careful not to have any provocation with the official leadership of the Tory Party who, we reckoned, would succumb to the temptation to 'dump us in the shit'.

As Julian Amery put it to me at our first tête-à-tête over lunch, 'I am more interested in saving the Union of Great Britain and Northern Ireland than advancing the cause of a Conservative Government.' Truth to tell, I felt just slightly guilty about my clandestine relations (on this one issue) for 20 years. That guilt evaporated when, during 1997–1998, I witnessed the extent to which Dewar and Company had 'got into bed' with the SNP.

Then there is also the phenomenon of 'short-termism', which has pervaded the upper echelons of the pro-Union, anti-SNP parties. 'It will go away like snow off a dyke, as quickly as it came,' Margaret Herbison told me. Chairman of the UK Labour Party and much loved by her North Lanarkshire constituents, Margaret genuinely believed that the SNP was a 'flash in the pan'. And, chatting to passers-by over her garden fence in her home mining village of Shotts, this miner's daughter, turned schoolteacher, was unassailable. Her successor, John Smith, MP for North Lanarkshire, did not have such a cosy, local relationship and, 20 years after his tragic death, it was no surprise to me whatsoever that industrially depleted North Lanarkshire was one of four areas to vote 'Yes' in the referendum. Herbison's situation and political position could be replicated throughout the 1960s by most Scottish MPs. Towards the end of the 1970s, short-termism stalked Westminster, Transport House and Smith Square. In 1976, during one of my weekly meetings with James Callaghan in my capacity as chairman of the Labour Party Foreign Affairs Group, I had told him that Ted Short's proposals for Scotland had 'all the durability of a plywood box'. 'Well,' he responded, 'a plywood box will last my political lifetime!' Pause and an arch-cynical chuckle. 'Maybe not yours, Tam!'

But perhaps the most significant reason Scots voters abandoned Labour in their droves in May 2015 can be summed up in just three words – Iraq and Afghanistan. The night in 2003 when we saw on television, bombs raining down from our bombers in an illuminated sky over Baghdad, a party member who had worked his butt off for me at five general elections came on the phone: 'I'm bloody well ashamed – I'm sitting on my bum while that bastard Blair remains Leader of the Labour Party.' He did and thousands like him. The truth is that, by the time of the Scottish Parliament elections in 2007, Labour Party activists, politically surly and increasingly thin on the ground, were just not prepared to work for foreign policies which were anathema to them. Scottish Labour activists tended to be seriously political, possibly more so than south of the border. One of the most difficult decisions of my public life was when I was approached by Welsh Nationalists and the SNP to join them in signing a motion suggesting that Blair be answerable for war crimes to the International Court at The Hague. I was sorely tempted to do so but was begged not to by parliamentary friends who felt equally strongly – Alice Mahon, John McDonnell, Neil Gerrard and Bob Marshall-Andrews – on the grounds that the narrative would move from the rights and wrongs of the Iraq War to Dalyell's treachery to the Labour Party.

Let me insert a personal judgement here. In 2003, at the outbreak of the Iraq War, Alex Salmond talked to me a lot at this time – partly because I had been to Iraq twice and had become a friend of Tariq Aziz, Saddam Hussein's Foreign Minister. Salmond and I, along with others who stridently opposed military action, were not at all popular. I believe he opposed the war because, deep inside him, he thought it was wrong. And I am absolutely certain that Jim Sillars, who, after he left the House of Commons, had worked in the Middle East, was genuinely outraged. He would phone me up and ask what on earth I or the Labour Party could do about the 'wicked' Blair and his spin doctor Alastair Campbell. Though they did not know it at the time, they – Salmond and Sillars – and the SNP were to be the beneficiaries of the left-wing anger which, either by abstention or by active support, propelled the SNP into power at Holyrood in 2007.

When the then Defence Secretary, John Reid, announced that British troops would join the Americans in Afghanistan, I reminded the House of Commons of Harold Macmillan's avuncular advice to his successor, Alec Douglas Home: 'Don't worry, old boy, you'll be all right – so long as you don't invade Afghanistan!' Reid was soon made to look ridiculous.

John Reid has many qualities as a politician. He was decisive. He was a 'can-doer' in several ministries. He was the most skilful of all the Labour government's contributors to BBC Radio 4's *Today* programme. He was one of the few who could fight a draw with John Humphrys or seemingly give an adequate answer to the subtly penetrating questions of James Naughtie. To my first-hand knowledge, in former Yugoslavia, he was superb at getting on the same wavelength with the troops. But the fact remains that many Scottish Labour Party activists, acquaintances from his days as a younger Communist and later as a researcher for the STUC, were cynical about the comrade they had known metamorphosing into the character they dubbed 'Field Marshal Reid'. This cynicism extended to other Scottish ministers. Many party activists judged that, if the Chancellor of the Exchequer, Gordon Brown, had put his foot down, Britain would not have joined Bush's invasions of Iraq or Afghanistan. That he did not do so was due to Brown's assessment – probably correct – that Blair would sack him, passing it off, as Macmillan had done when Peter Thorneycroft, Enoch Powell, and Nigel Birch resigned as Treasury ministers in 1958, as a 'little local difficulty'. Alistair Darling was characteristically candid. If he had started kicking up the dust over Iraq, it would have no effect on Blair–Bush policies and would simply mean his exit from the Cabinet, to no purpose, when he was doing constructive work in other departments.

The cumulative effect of all these factors on the part of the Scottish Labour leadership was that the party members became lethargic and handed the political narrative to the SNP on a plate.

In a situation where the SNP won 56 out of 59 Scottish seats in the British Parliament, it is seductive for 'Men of the Union', like me, to squeal that it is unfair on the grounds that the 50 per cent who did not vote for the SNP deserve to be represented. After all, majorities have rights – at least in a democracy they do. I decline to be seduced by the argument that because the SNP have 56 out of 59 MPs there is an argument for PR, on account of two things.

First, over 43 years as MP for West Lothian, I held 48 surgeries each year and addressed, I reckon, some 3,500 significant individual grievances, involving government departments. It became clear to me that it was hugely important that those harbouring grievances, be they either individual constituents, organisations or local businesses, should be in no doubt, to whom they should go. As US president Harry S. Truman put it, 'The buck stops with me.' Observing the buck passing that takes place when individuals approach both directly elected and list members of the Scottish Parliament convinces me that a system of identifiable individual representative has huge merit. I have witnessed how Labour voters go to a Labour list MSP, rather than their directly elected SNP MSP – and vice versa. Confusion delays remedies of grievance.

My second objection to PR is also rooted in experience. Between 1976 and 1979, I was a member of the indirectly elected

European Parliament. My main work was on the Committee on Budgets and the subcommittee of the Budgets Committee, the equivalent of the Public Accounts Committee of the House of Commons. My Budgets Committee chairman was the brave Erwin Lange – he had been allocated to the SS Punishment Brigade in 1942 in Russia for his socialist views. He represented industrial Essen in the Bundestag. On several occasions, I went to Lange on sticky issues to ask him what we should do about them. His answer was always the same – he would have to consult Herbert Wehner. Wehner was the thuggish, ex-Communist floor leader in the Bundestag in Bonn. Erwin explained that Wehner determined members' places on the list and, if he crossed him, he would be so far down the list that he would not be re-elected to the European Parliament. Erwin said it was terrible but that was just the way of things.

In October 2015, I learned that the committee to look at the constitution, set up by the new Labour leader, Jeremy Corbyn, under the chairmanship of his friend and mine, Jon Trickett MP,[2] was veering towards a federal solution. Indeed, a federal solution has appealed to many serious and constructive people, particularly within the Liberal Party and its former leaders, David Steel and Menzies Campbell. I harbour doubts.

There remains a huge difficulty with federalism – it will not go away. It lies in the way the population of the UK is divided, with some 87 per cent in England and 13 per cent in

---

2   Trickett was appointed to the newly created post of Shadow Minister for the Constitutional Convention on 14 September 2015.

Scotland, Wales and Northern Ireland. I have a further difficulty. I wonder what thought has been given to the complications and expense of setting up a federal parliament, essential to any such federation. But, in relation to Scotland, there is yet another difficulty. The leaders of the SNP are simply not interested in a federal solution. Their cause is, as it has always been, an independent Scottish state. It is ridiculous to pretend otherwise.

And those in favour of a federal state had better be careful what they wish for. In a federal state, the central government, by codified law, cannot alter the powers of the constituent regions. Such powers are enshrined in a constitution. Any disputes would be resolved by a supreme or constitutional court. So disputes – and they would be numerous and often acrimonious – between Holyrood and Westminster would be questions of law for resolution in a court. Emphatically they would *not* be questions of politics to be addressed by politicians in inter-governmental negotiations. Let us be clear – federalism would mean an end to the sovereignty of the UK Parliament. And, incidentally, federalism would also mean an end to the 'sovereignty of the Scottish people' – a slogan much bandied around at the time of the Claim of Right in 1989 and indeed in the 2014 referendum – because they would be beholden to an overarching federal parliament. And, apart from anything else, disputes would inevitably mean more time and energy being spent on political wrangling rather than on governing – the curse of so many administrations.

In my view, Scotland has never ceased to be a nation and its national rights were enshrined in the Union of the Crowns

(1603) and the Union of the Parliament (1707), when the United Kingdom came into being. The subsequent constitutional arrangements have been a matter for much argument over the years and continue to be so.

If a tier of government, based on the concept of the 'nation' – Donald Dewar's oft-used chosen word – was created, it is inevitable that, sooner rather than later, a nationalist party would get the job of running it, despite Labour's assumption that is would always be the party of government in Scotland. Foreseeable and foreseen, predictable and predicted, this outcome was as plain as a pikestaff to George Cunningham and me in 1978–79. Left to themselves, it is hardly to be doubted that eventually the members of the Holyrood Parliament would agitate for a wholly independent Scottish state. Cynically, they would, at first, acquiesce in divorce and the fracturing of the United Kingdom. Why should anyone believe that the SNP would have an interest in making anything short of independence work?

These problems all came to a head in the referendum of 18 September 2014. As with any binary question, it created a polarisation – in communities that did not want to be polarised. It was divisive, often bitter. A 'once in a generation' referendum (as we were told this one would be by Alex Salmond) should be a matter of law, not a matter for the First Minister (or her predecessors) randomly to determine. But when a subordinate parliament is set up, as the Scottish Parliament was, in some haste, to appease the rising tide of nationalism, some of its powers allow subjective interpretation, such as the ability to alter regulations in relation to the safety of medicines.

'Nicola Sturgeon . . . thinks that David Cameron has "no right" to say that there will be no second referendum . . .

However [at the 2015 general election] an . . . insight [was given] into the thinking of the SNP. Let's say that the vote has nothing to do with independence. Then demand that we alone decide on having a second referendum, when we get most Scottish seats on a false promise.'3

So haunting Scotland now is the vexed question of whether there will be yet another referendum. Forget all those statements scattered around in August and September 2014 about the referendum being 'once in a generation'. Only the most gullible ever gave credence to such pledges. And, to be fair, a number of those in the Yes campaign were careful to insert that 'any material changes' would allow them to escape from a pledge not to campaign for another referendum, if the 'No' campaign won. The 2015 election result, the SNP are claiming, constitutes just such a 'material change'. The reality is that whether the Scottish government propose one or not will be entirely for the SNP's own internal calculations.

In the spring of 2016 I doubted whether the question the SNP asked itself was: 'Is another referendum good or bad for Scotland?' I fear the question was: 'Can we win another overall majority at Holyrood with a proposal for another referendum in the 2016 manifesto for elections to the Scottish Parliament?' If I am correct, I can only stare into the abyss of years of constitutional conflict and deepening societal division. I am reconciled to the reality that the question was entirely decided according to the perceived electoral interests of the SNP.

---

3   'Have your Say', *The Scotsman*, 14 May 2015, reply from Andrew HN Gray, Edinburgh, to the question 'David Cameron doesn't want to be the Prime Minister responsible for the break-up of the UK so how best does he preserve the Union?'.

The constant possibility of another referendum is dangerously destabilising. It might be wise at this point to pay heed to the Canadian experience. In 1972, Jack Cunningham, then MP for Whitehaven in Cumbria, and I, weekly columnist for *New Scientist*, were invited to visit Canada by the nuclear authorities of Ontario and Québec who were immensely proud of their CANDU reactors at Bruce and Pickering. Leaving Ontario, Cunningham and I went to the nuclear power stations at Gentilly and Trois-Rivières. At the end of the day, after climbing ladders and hearing explanations of dials in operation rooms, the engineers invited us to a convivial dinner. We were taken aback by the ferocity of the argument between our hosts, some of whom wanted to remain in the Canadian entity and others who wanted French/francophone Canada to hive off from Ottawa. The events of the ensuing 40 years may offer something of a warning to Scotland. Cunningham and I were not at all surprised a few years later to learn that there was to be a referendum on independence. The result, in 1980, went 60–40 against the separatists. But the Parti Québécois remained in charge of the government. It took them a decade and a half to risk another referendum, which, in 1995, they lost by the narrowest of margins and against all expectations. In 2014, the Québec nationalists proposed a third referendum but they suffered a decisive electoral rejection. The history is that Québec lived for 40 years with exactly the single-issue source of political division that is now in grave danger of becoming the norm in Scotland. Over this period of time, the Province of Québec suffered severe economic damage – to say nothing of deep and destructive hostility between nationalists and those opposed to nationalism, with which we in Scotland are becoming all too familiar. And, consider this – in 1972 when Cunningham and I went to Canada, Montreal, the venue of Expo '67, and Toronto were roughly equal – Montreal perhaps having the edge commercially. In 2015, Toronto is streets ahead, as a major city of Canada. The Edinburgh financial community could well find itself in a similar situation to Montreal. What the government Ottawa did not fully understand was the leadership of the Parti Québécois's 'strength of conviction' – just as, even yet, Whitehall, I fear, has not fully come to terms with the 'strength of conviction' of the SNP leadership.

Although the SNP's share of the vote in 2015 was 50 per cent, I still maintain that the natural hard core 'Nat' vote is between 25 and 30 per cent.[4] The First Minister is simply doing what she and her SNP colleagues so often do – equating their supporters with the people of Scotland, as if the rest of us do not exist and do not have an equally patriotic and deeply held, albeit different, view of what constitutional arrangement is in the best interests of our country. It is far from certain that a majority of the electorate would support a 'Yes' vote in another referendum.

The reality is also that many of those who voted 'Yes' in the referendum and who voted SNP in May 2015 shudder at the prospect of another referendum in the near future. The reason is not far to seek. The prospect of yet another referendum and

---

4   I believe the dramatic rise in SNP membership after the No vote can be put down in large part to the extraordinary camaraderie that developed between pro-independence supporters during the long run-up to the referendum, fuelled, in no small part, by the potency of social media.

its consequent uncertainties has a seeping detrimental effect on business and investment decisions. Business hates uncertainty and I can think of no other more damaging situation than the constant threat of a referendum which would have vast consequences for the people of Scotland, for it would most certainly have an impact on the long-term future of investment in Scotland, not only on the part of investors from England and abroad, but also on the part of Scots ourselves. I doubt if there will be any dramatic announcement to the effect that investment will be withheld or shift elsewhere, on account of the extra powers being offered by Holyrood. No, it is far more likely that companies who might have thought of investing in Scotland would plan to do so elsewhere. The Scottish economy depends significantly on being part of the larger UK market. It should be obvious to anyone that businesses will choose to locate to where the larger part of their market is to be found.

16

A 'Citizen of the United Kingdom'

❖

So what of the future? With 56 Westminster MPs (now reduced to 54), the SNP voice is strong but their claim to speak for all Scotland is preposterous.

As I have already said, I believe many of those who voted SNP at the 2015 general election – the majority, I would say – want Scotland to remain in the United Kingdom. Yet the SNP leadership, since the 2015 general election, suppose that they have the right to pass legislation, relating to Scotland, from the opposition benches. In the summer of 2015, it seemed that every SNP amendment that was defeated should have been interpreted as an affront to Scotland. Pro-Union MPs are accused not only of talking Scotland down but voting the country down too.

With 54 of their MPs at Westminster, some of the SNP seemed to be suggesting that the voice of Scotland would now be heard at Westminster for the first time. I find this both preposterously untrue and profoundly offensive – it denies the commitment and hard work done to promote and protect Scottish interests of many MPs over the years. Within months of my election to Parliament, Alec Douglas-Home

(MP for Kinross and Western Perthshire) was to move from the post of an authoritative and influential Foreign Secretary into Number 10 Downing Street. He was to be Foreign Secretary again from 1970 to 1974 and I was told by Geoffrey Rippon, the Cabinet Minister who did the day-to-day negotiations on EEC entry, that Home remained a 'vastly influential member of Ted Heath's inner group'. My first Secretary of State for Scotland, Jack Maclay, Viscount Muirshiel (MP for West Renfrewshire), really mattered in the Macmillan Cabinet, as did his successor, Michael Noble, Baron Glenkinglas (MP for Argyll). Tom Fraser, who was succeeded at Hamilton by Winnie Ewing, was a key ally of Hugh Gaitskell, in the Shadow Cabinet, and Peggy Herbison was Chairman of the UK Labour Party. Later in the 1960s, Harold Wilson deferred to Willie Ross.

Even more absurd is the idea that the voice of Scotland did not ring out in the Liberal Party or Liberal Democrats. For Heaven's sake, the party had four Scottish or Scottish-anchored leaders – Jo Grimond, David Steel, Charles Kennedy and Menzies Campbell – to say nothing of effective long-serving MPs, such as Russell Johnston, leader of the Scottish Liberal Party and deputy leader of the Liberal Democrats (who played an important role in Europe), Michael Moore and Alistair Carmichael.

The 54 SNP MPs should be true to the promises made by Nicola Sturgeon during her the general election campaign. I respect the democratic will of the Scottish people who sent them to Westminster – but they were not sent there to fester with secessionist sentiment or to promote the nationalist agenda of their party. They were sent to represent their constituents in the Parliament of the United Kingdom and ultimately to work for the benefit of the entirety of the British people and the strong role of the Scots within that Union. But I fear that the hard core is unappeasable.

But so much depends on attitude and a willingness to work together. I was appalled to hear the MP for Linlithgow and East Falkirk, Martyn Day, had concluded his maiden speech in the House of Commons by saying that he would enjoy his term in London 'behind enemy lines'. Intended to be flippant or not, it fosters an impression of hostility. I prefer to think that even many of those who voted SNP in the May 2015 election would not care to think of their elected representative in the British Parliament to be working 'behind enemy lines'.

Hitherto, this book has been – yes, I confess – the personal chronicle of the events by which the kingdom of Great Britain and Northern Ireland metamorphosed into the fractured state it is currently in and it is written by one of the few political participants in those events who is still alive. When I first entered Parliament in the 1960s, that kingdom had seemed to be impregnable.

Whether I like it or not – and, actually, I do not – the Scottish Parliament in Edinburgh will exist at least for some years to come and certainly past the time when I and my contemporaries are all gone. The members and not only those of the SNP persuasion but of all political hues – Green, Labour, Liberal, Tory – will continue to complain that they have insufficient powers and insufficient money from the Treasury in London. It is an eternal truth that elected politicians crave ever more powers for the institution to which they themselves are elected. It is fanciful to think that the appetite of Holyrood can ever be assuaged other than by full independence. Yet, despite what many SNP supporters mouth and what the party would have us believe, the SNP leadership must be ever-more apprehensive about the unpopularity which would accrue to them as a result of cuts they would be forced to make in the event of severance from the UK.

Bearing this in mind, what would happen if there was another referendum in the foreseeable future? And supposing it becomes clear that, once again, the majority do not support the break-up of Britain, what should become of the Holyrood Parliament? Perhaps it would chunter on for some years and then wither away, dying a slow death. A hugely unlikely claim, bordering on the preposterous? Well, not quite. Of course the MSPs would be outraged at the prospect and some journalists dismissive. Yet, the reaction of local elected councillors, who are required to deliver the services about which Holyrood legislates, might not be. Many local councillors, already resentful of the centralising tendencies of Holyrood, are incandescent with anger at what they perceive to be the rapidly increasing costs of the Scottish Government and Holyrood. A cavalcade of first ministers, assorted Cabinet secretaries, ministers and MSPs do the same job, I think, less well and at vastly more expense than was done when I was first elected to the House of Commons. Looking back, Jack Maclay, Priscilla, Lady Tweedsmuir, Gordon Campbell, Ian MacArthur and Gilmour Leburn and, subsequently, Willie Ross, Dick Mabon, Judith Hart and Norman Buchan all did sterling work in the Scottish Office.

From the perspective of better provision of public services, it has, alas, become only too clear that the devolution experiment on this island has failed, not just in Edinburgh but in Cardiff too. All the chatter of more powers, fewer powers and use of existing powers has not improved by one jot the ineffectual governance which we have been subject to since 1999.

Contrast the soaring expense of Holyrood, the Scottish Cabinet ministers, their host of advisers and additional civil servants, members of the Scottish Parliament and their researchers with the dire plight of little Argyll and Bute Council. No different from other local authorities, they are at the end of their tether. Argyll and Bute are having to turf over their beds of roses and other public floral displays as part of efforts to save £18 million over two years. Flowers have been targeted because of the relatively high cost of maintaining and cultivating the beds, which the council estimates would save £100,000 a year. The Christmas lights are to be axed to save a further £100,000. Infinitely more important, education will be hit with 72 additional support assistants sacked to save £1.4 million. Other measures include a 50 per cent increase in musical tuition fees, burial and cremation costs increased by 20 per cent, and waste collection reduced to once every three weeks. Such grim necessities are universal among Scottish local authorities but do not reflect the overall position in England.

When it permeates through to the Scottish electorate that financial provision for education, health, policing and social welfare is increasingly unsatisfactory in comparison with provision south of the border, the 'Scottish people' will start pointing their collective finger at Holyrood and desire to return to robust local government, where democracy and accountability are closer to the people.

❖

I am a citizen of the United Kingdom. I have freedom of worship, speech, association and expression. The Scots have shared a common culture with the English, Irish and Welsh since even before the Act of Union in 1707. In the modern globalised world, the notion that one of the most prosperous and relatively influential states in the world could break down into its constituent nations seems preposterous and unnecessary. And even more so, considering the issue was settled by referendum in September 2014. But yet we are living through an age of the most profound constitutional crisis in the history of these islands.

However, I do see some rays of hope and a vision for the future. It is not a vision which would have us to return to the past – the events of the last decades cannot be undone. At heart it involves some pragmatic advice to the party which I served as MP for almost half a century in answer to the pressing question: 'What can the Labour Party in Scotland do to re-assert itself?' I have a very succinct view. Eschew current notions of Labour in Scotland forming a detached organisation from the British Labour Party. Stick firmly and proudly with the British Labour Party. Furthermore, party members should be calm and remain patient. The SNP is as much a church as it is a conventional political party – and the congregation has, so far, trusted its ministers. So far, faith has trumped reason. When the congregation discovers that those ministers cannot deliver their promises, as will inevitably be the case, the SNP government will be vulnerable and probably subject to mighty wrath. Douglas Alexander, who lost in Paisley in 2015 told me, 'It was like fighting fog.' Fog has a habit of dispersing.

But the fog did not disperse before the 2016 Scottish parliamentary elections despite Nicola Sturgeon's appeal to her party faithful during their conference in Inverness in autumn 2015 to 'judge us on our record'. But what is that record? The truth is that, in the past eight years, in the devolved matters of health, education, the police and fire service, the SNP have presided over a catastrophic decline

The Scottish National Health Service is in crisis. Targets for cancer treatments are woefully unmet. More than 1,000 beds have been closed in Scottish hospitals since 2012. Expenditure in the NHS in Scotland in 2014 fell by 1.2 per cent. In England, it rose by 4.4 per cent. Education on training midwives and nurses in Scotland has been cut by 1,190 places. And there has been an alarming decline in GP provision. In many cases, difficulty in making urgent appointments has resulted in the deterioration in medical conditions. Anecdotal evidence suggests that generally – it varies from health authority to health authority – accident and emergency problems have been addressed more quickly and to greater effect in England.

In education, the SNP government pledged to limit primary school class sizes to a maximum of 18 – a pledge it made when it first came into government in 2007. In fact, class sizes have risen in every one of the last five years, reaching 25 in some cases. Relations between my professional association – I am a paid-up member of the Educational Institute of Scotland – and the SNP Government are cryogenic.

In education, the stark truth is that, under the Scottish government, there has been a real drop in literacy and numeracy standards as evidenced in the S5 and S6 exam results. Figures from the Scottish Survey of Literacy and Numeracy endorse the statistic that Scotland is at a severe disadvantage to England. I think there was also an element of deceit. The figures were available to Scottish ministers in

April 2016. They were not made public until after the election
of May 2016. And the problem that the universities face is
that schools serving deprived areas are simply not producing
enough students to enable universities to meet the much-
trumpeted aspirations of the government. The government in
Edinburgh, while boasting about free tuition fees (made
possible by the Barnett formula) have introduced significant
cuts in the grants for poor students. And the government in
Edinburgh have made cuts to teacher numbers and education
spending which, of course, led to the decline in literacy and
numeracy.

The SNP have trumpeted slogans about free tuition fees.
In fact, university students have been saddled with greater
debt because they have to start repaying their loans once
their incomes reach £16,500, while the figure in England in
2015 is £21,000. As Rector of Edinburgh University between
2003 and 2006 and as an Honorary Doctor of St Andrews,
Heriot-Watt and Napier, my contacts tell me of a concerning
drift of talented colleagues to universities in England.

Wickedly – and I have chosen the word carefully – part-
time college places have been cut by 130,000. If Scotland is
to be a fairer society, this appalling situation must be reversed.
If Scotland is to prosper, we need skilled men and women
with precisely the skills that can be acquired through part-
time study. There is nothing fair about trumpeting free tuition
fees for university students while, at the same time, depriving
less academic students of the opportunity to participate in
shorter-term courses.

Most alarming also is the saga of the delayed payments to
farmers from the Common Agricultural Policy. This is not the
place to detail the circumstances, which drove the NFU to
despair. Sufficient to say that the culpability of the Scottish

Government was such that it provoked the European Commission to issue a fine of £125 million.

Caroline Gardiner, Auditor General for Scotland has expressed 'serious concerns' over the Scottish Governments's response to the problems. She said: 'The scale of the challenge ahead should not be underestimated. It is vital that the Scottish Government takes steps to ensure the IT system is fit for purpose and fully addresses the potential financial impact if it is unable to meet the Commission's regulations.' Her report revealed that Richard Lochhead, the Agriculture minister, had failed to meet a series of key targets. He pledged that 25 per cent of farmers would be paid by the end of December 2015, but the actual figure was much lower.

The SNP policy regarding the police has been no less catastrophic. Contrary to advice from senior figures in the police and Police Federation, the SNP government insisted, with the connivance of Sir Stephen House, then Chief Constable of Strathclyde, in creating a single Scottish police force. It has been an unmitigated disaster. Local community policing has suffered with officers being assigned to duties in areas where they have little or no experience. And, I have yet to meet a serving police officer who is in favour of a national force. We never sought to encounter the sight of armed policemen performing routine duties on the streets of Glasgow. Let us return to regional police forces.

With the election of my friend in Labour Party adversity, Jeremy Corbyn, the future direction of Politics in Scotland may be different. I was pleasantly surprised that Corbyn was able to squeeze the required 35 MPs required to put him on the ballot paper for leader. I was entirely unsurprised that, once on the ballot paper, Corbyn gained a resounding victory.

Along with Corbyn, I had been one of the ignored who had pleaded with Blair not to go to war in Iraq and bomb Baghdad. Two of the other contenders for the party leadership, Andy Burnham and Yvette Cooper, had meekly acquiesced in policies which have brought mayhem to the Middle East. As for Liz Kendall, she had been dubbed with the toxic label of 'Blairite', as far as the Labour electorate in 2015 were concerned.

There were two other reasons for Corbyn's success. I had worked closely with him on the issue of the wicked treatment by successive British governments of the Chagos Islanders, expelled from their Indian Ocean atoll in June 1967 to make way for the American base at Diego Garcia. It was then that I first noticed Corbyn was good with civil servants, in that he listened courteously and put our case rationally.

Some years ago, I was invited as a supper guest speaker to the Islington North Labour Party. It was obvious to me that Jeremy Corbyn inspired real affection as well as respect among his multi-ethnic constituents. Both respect and affection are commodities that are desperately needed in a leader of the Labour Party.

So it was my hope that he and his inner group – John McDonnell in particular – would work with the SNP in Parliament. Of course, I understood that English and Welsh members of the Parliamentary Labour Party might harbour a visceral reluctance to work with SNP members who had slaughtered their Scottish friends, comrades and colleagues of the previous parliament. But sometimes there can be a merging of personal considerations.

I had also hoped that the majority of SNP MPs, all the

better for coming from actual jobs in the community – rather than the all-too-common background of school, higher education, researcher to some more senior politician, special adviser to a minister and MP – would settle down and exercise their judgement in the best interests of Britain, while not abandoning their Scottish concerns. Of course, they are entitled to campaign for independence, whenever there is a clear appetite for another referendum.

For me, the Union is partly a matter of gut emotion but it is far more than that. The Union is about the pooling and sharing of risk and resources. The Union is about solidarity – especially in the circumstances of adversity. The Union is about standing together on social security.

The Union is about having a single economic framework which gives us Scots a domestic market ten times the size of Scotland, with whom to trade, to live and work in. The Union is about being a place to which Scots and English may choose to work or retire anywhere within Britain, without any impediment at all.

The Union is about collective defence. As a national serviceman in the Royal Scots Greys (1950–52) or, as we must now call them since amalgamation, the Royal Scots Dragoon Guards, I shared a Centurion tank with two English lads and a lad from Swansea. It is madness to think of unpicking today's infinitely more sophisticated British Army on the basis of nationality and oblivious of technical training. How does Scotland have one tenth of an aircraft carrier? Are we to be allocated a couple of Tornadoes with separate engineering backup and maintenance?

I am a Man of the Union because the alternative is puerile, romantic folly. I doubt if the SNP non-zealots and the sitting-on-the-fence commentariat (news pundits) have any notion as to what the dismantling of the United Kingdom and the disentangling of Scotland from England, not least over tax, in practical terms, actually entail.

We need to create ways of making the Union really matter to people, of making it come alive, of showing people how it makes a real difference to their lives, before we lose it all by default. Only if the United Kingdom was to be fractured and we had all gone our separate ways would we come to appreciate what had been lost.

Epilogue

❖

The Question of Scotland is not – and does not pretend to be – a commentary on the situation as it looks at a particular point in time such as June 2016. It is one participant's perspective of how on earth events unfolded in such a way that the Kingdom of Great Britain and Northern Ireland has arrived at a fractured constitutional position that would have been unthinkable to most people – though not to me – half a century earlier.

The results of the 2016 election for the Scottish Parliament were predictable and predicted, foreseeable and foreseen. I feel in the slightly uncomfortable position of an elderly 83-year-old grandfather waving his stick at the new generation. But, dear, oh dear, the 2016 election campaign did plumb new depths of inconsequentiality. One abiding memory is of opening Scottish newspapers on Saturday, 23 April, to see pictures of the leader of the Conservative Party in Scotland, Ruth Davidson, clinging for dear life on to the back of a bemused buffalo. What was the political message? That, as a Scottish Tory, Ms Davidson was feisty enough to be Leader of the Opposition? All right, in 1979, Margaret Thatcher, we seem to remember, did have an adventure with a calf but then I go back to my first three Tory prime ministers – Harold MacMillan, Alec Douglas-Home and Ted Heath. Ted Heath astride a buffalo? I think not – the imagination boggles. Politics is demeaned.

The serious point is that gravitas in politics has been diluted. What seems to count is not so much the political context of what they, the political party leaders, are saying but how they look standing behind an artificial podium, reacting at the behest of a quizmasterly Glen Campbell or Sarah Smith of BBC Scotland or Bernard Ponsonby of STV. Moreover, I am very uncomfortable when I witness the lengths to which the leaders of the Tory and Labour Parties in Scotland are prepared to distance themselves from their parties in England.

And, yet and yet . . . The UK national press collectively swooned at Ms Davidson's achievement. Some went as far as to suggest that this kickboxing, buffalo-riding, intrepid young woman was well qualified to be David Cameron's successor as prime minister – preposterous – but the electors would seem to have endorsed this.

It seems to have worked at the polls. Yes, Ruth Davidson did indeed win the Scottish parliamentary seat of Edinburgh Central. But I know a great many people in Edinburgh Central. I am quite certain that it was not on account of her buffalo-riding or kickboxing skills or the cascade of photo opportunities that they cast their votes for her. It was because she was the most likely candidate to preserve the Union with England.

Certainly, there seemed little likelihood that the Labour Party would achieve that. Their leader in Scotland, Kezia Dugdale, admitted that, should Brexit come to pass, it was 'not inconceivable' she would back independence and she would allow her MSPs to campaign for independence in the event of another referendum. The effect of this was that any Labour supporters in favour of keeping the Union – and that will not be an insignificant number – could feel that the only place that they could go is to the Tories.

Scottish Labour's woes have been brought about by the well-perceived confusion on the constitutional question. Some would vote 'Yes' to an independent Scotland in a referendum. Others would vote 'No'. Kezia Dugdale gave the impression that she was relaxed one way or the other – party policy was to let each individual choose how they should vote, which is fair enough. However, electors are entitled to be given a lead from their party of choice as to what the party policy on the issue itself is. Many erstwhile Labour voters instinctively sensed that the break-up of Britain is a subject about which we cannot be relaxed. Personally, I am sorry for Kezia Dugdale and her colleagues in that – as this book chronicles – the seeds of their misfortune were sown decades before.

Ruth Davidson (Leader of the Scottish Conservatives), Kezia Dugdale (Leader of Scottish Labour), Patrick Harvie (Co-Convenor of the Scottish Green Party) and Willie Rennie (Leader of the Scottish Liberal Democrats) are all talented and agreeable human beings, with principles and beliefs, but the cumulative effect of their nightly TV appearances led to the unattractive impression of it being all about me, me, me, me – the cult of valuing personality over party policy and the way the importance of the individual has come to matter more than a unified party manifesto backed by potential ministers in any elected government.

Why did we not see more, much more, of the party leaders' senior colleagues? To focus just on my own party, could we not have seen more of the deputy leader, Alex Rowley, the

MSP for Lothian, Neil Findlay, the MSP for Dumbarton, Jackie Baillie, and the MSP for North East Scotland, Jenny Marra, for example?

One of the best formats of recent years has been 'Election Call', part of *World at One* on BBC Radio 4. It featured listeners putting pertinent, probing questions to the big beasts of each party and a good deal of political light emerged from their responses. In contrast to this, the new-style podium scrums on TV feature politicians trying to score cheap points off each other. It seems to me to be all about style over substance and it allows the messages politicians are trying to get across to the electorate to go unchallenged. I am less than astonished by Nicola Sturgeon's current electoral success. I find the de facto presidential contest out of tune with politics in Britain.

But – and it is a very big but indeed – electoral success in 2016 does not mean that the SNP will achieve their ostensible political aim of separation from the rest of the UK in a referendum. I suspect – it can only be a suspicion – that Nicola Sturgeon and her husband, Peter Murrell, share my view that, in the foreseeable future, saying 'Yes' to independence would not win. And Ms Sturgeon is, I judge, far too wily a politician to embark on holding a referendum that she thinks she might not win. Indeed, my political nostrils in Scotland tell me that the advantage to the 'No' vote, were there to be a referendum in 2016/17, would not be 55 per cent to 45 per cent as was the outcome in 2014, but closer to 65 per cent to 35 per cent. And that remains my view even after the results of the referendum on EU membership of June 2016. Low oil prices would influence the vote but it's not just about oil prices – the creeping centralisation of government is yet another factor.

Understandably, people ask me, 'Mr Dalyell, what would you do?' And my answer? My preferred solution would be to terminate the parliament in Edinburgh. This is manifestly unrealistic in the current climate. There would be fury from (not quite all) MSPs, outrage from the Scottish-based journalists and antagonism from BBC Scotland and STV. Nor can I see the Westminster government grasping the nettle and bringing the parliament in Edinburgh to an end – even though it is undoubtedly in their power to do so. But surely we could move towards a more democratic position by returning powers to the local authorities, whose councillors are at their wits' end as to how to finance the delivery of services to their communities. It sticks in councillors' gullets that they have to make unfair cutbacks while the vastly expensive Holyrood and its whole paraphernalia of personal research assistants and support staff for members' offices continue to cost more by the year. In my view, the ministers in Holyrood do less satisfactorily and more expensively what, as Secretary of State for Scotland, Jack Maclay, Michael Noble, Willie Ross, Gordon Campbell and Bruce Millan did with a handful of junior ministers.

Real devolution should be to the regions. This would bring decision making and accountability as close as possible to the people, as the 1969 'Wheatley Report', published by the Royal Commission on Local Government in Scotland, spelt out in detail. Let Glasgow and most of what was Strathclyde follow Greater Manchester. If an institution like Holyrood is set up on the basis of nationality, can we be surprised that its members will demand more and more, until it either achieves independence or is dissolved? Pandora's box was opened before its contents could be scrutinised due to the ruthless and wicked decision of Brown, Dewar,

McLeish and their entourage to impose a guillotine so that their proposals for Scotland went unexamined.

Between 1998 and 1999, during the passage of The Scotland Bill, I did my best to alert colleagues to the need to have sufficient parliamentary time to discuss what was an important constitutional issue. The tradition of the British Parliament was that constitutional bills should not be guillotined and that there were sound and tested reasons for this position. I wonder how many people now recollect this?

From a distance – 11 years have gone by since I left a very different House of Commons – I confess to being impressed by the contribution of many Westminster MPs of the SNP group. Most of them have had 'real' jobs and have not trodden the path of school to university to someone's researcher to special adviser to somebody else and in to the House – up the 'greasy poll'. In particular, for example, I applaud the attitude of Philippa Whitford, SNP MP for Central Ayrshire, who continues to work as a surgeon. My first whip, John Cronin, Labour MP for Loughborough (1955–79), also practised surgery three mornings a week and turned up in the House in the afternoon.

Am I allowed just to wonder how many of the Westminster SNP MPs are still as enthusiastic about Holyrood and the break-up of Britain?

On 28 October 1971, Bill Rodgers, Shirley Williams, Dick Taverne and I, along with 65 other Labour MPs, defied a Labour Party three-line whip, following a debate in the House of Commons about Britain becoming part of the European Union. The 69 Labour MPs who joined the Conservatives in Edward Heath's lobby ensured the motion in favour was carried and I have never repented doing so. But, from this position, I did wonder again whether opinion in Scotland on

Brexit was really so very different from that in England. But in the event, at the 2016 referendum, this proved not to be the case.

In July 1962, aged twenty-nine, and six weeks old as an MP, I sauntered into the Members' Dining Room of the Commons at 12.35 p.m. It was empty, other than one old gentleman sitting alone at a table for two. I asked if I could join him. 'Sit down,' he said. It was (Earl) Clement Attlee, Churchill's War Time Deputy-Prime Minister and Labour Prime Minister, 1945–1951. Famously laconic, his first piece of advice was: 'Young man, keep out of the House of Commons Bars.' (I never did venture in for a drink.) After the soup, he said: 'What you owe the country, the Parliamentary Labour Party and your West Lothian Constituency Labour Party, is your best judgement.'

I am told by my friend and political opponent (in that order of priority), Ken Clarke, former Chancellor of the Exchequer, that, as I write in June 2016, there are more than a hundred Tory MPs wandering around, dazed, desperately wanting to remain in Europe, but hesitant to deny the 'mantra' – his word – of the will of the people. I know from other political friends and colleagues that the majority of the Parliamentary Labour Party and all Liberals are in a similar position, and 54 SNP MPs are committed to an outcome whereby at least Scotland remains in Europe.

Back to Clement Attlee and his advice to me. Do not these MPs have a duty, no less, to oppose the triggering of a divorce from Europe? I have it on the authority of two former Clerks of the Commons, Sir William McKay and Sir Robert Rodgers, that the relationship between Parliament and Referendum results has never been codified, but that most certainly the House of Commons is sovereign.

MPs should have the balls to say and vote for what they deem right for their country, on such an important issue, for young people and generations to come in particular.

Insurrections by 'Leave' Campaigners? Probably. But, in my opinion containable, as many people who voted 'Leave' come to realise the implications of divorce from Europe that they did not fully seem to appreciate when they voted. Any civil disorder will be as nothing as to when tens of thousands discover that their jobs are vanishing as a result of denial of access to the single European Market – access that Vote Leave in May/June 2016 told us was 'assured'.

Time and again in the pages of *The Question of Scotland* the issue of cowardice rears its head. This book, in July 2016, calls on MPs not to be political cowards, and vote for what they believe is best for Britain.

Postscript

❖

THIS HISTORY IS very much a personal one. That of course means that much is about the Labour Party and its actions. But the failure to confront nationalism lies across all parties. It is the belief of rational men and women that an emotional grievance can be assuaged by a rational response. It cannot be assuaged, it can only be fed, and each feed that it receives strengthens and validates it for the next attack. It is late in the day but, if this book helps those of us who believe that the Union is much greater than the sum of its parts and much lessened by the division of those parts, then it will have done some good for that cause. It is ironic that nationalism is allowed to find its voice through the fundamental human rights and freedoms guaranteed and created by the same state it seeks to destroy. It claims to be the sole representation of Scotland when the country it seeks to break was largely built by Scots, governed by Scots with a belief system generated by Scots. It is always easy for the political huckster to play the emotional card to disguise intellectual bankruptcy. But the most powerful arguments are those that spring not from emotion or reason but from the harnessing of both in a cause. We Men and Women of the Union have that cause. We need to find that voice.

The German philosopher Schopenhauer sums nationalism up succinctly:

> The cheapest sort of pride is national pride; for if a man is proud of his own nation, it argues that he has no qualities of his own of which he can be proud; otherwise he would not have recourse to those which he shares with so many millions of his fellow men. The man who is endowed with important personal qualities will be only too ready to see clearly in what respects his own nation falls short, since their failings will be constantly before his eyes. But every miserable fool who has nothing at all of which he can be proud adopts, as a last resource, pride in the nation to which he belongs; he is ready and glad to defend all its faults and follies tooth and nail, thus reimbursing himself for his own inferiority.

Let these words stand as an epitaph for this book.

Index

❖